Keeping Chickens as Pets.

Keeping Chickens in Your Backyard.
A Beginner's Guide

by

Ernest Eshott

ALL RIGHTS RESERVED. This book contains material protected under International and Federal Copyright Laws and Treaties.

Any unauthorized reprint or use of this material is strictly prohibited. No part of this book may be reproduced or transmitted in any form or by any means, electronic, mechanical or otherwise, including photocopying or recording, or by any information storage and retrieval system without express written permission from the author.

Copyrighted © 2014

Published by: IMB Publishing

Table of Contents

Table of Contents

Table of Contents 3

Introduction 7

   History of Chickens 7

Chapter 1 : Life Stages 12

   1) Roosters 12

   2) Capons 13

   3) Hens 13

   4) Eggs 14

   5) Embryo Development 15

   6) Chicks 15

   7) Point of Lay 16

Chapter 2: Anatomy 17

   1) Parts of a Chicken 17

   2) Feathers 20

   3) Markings 22

   4) Combs 23

Chapter 3: The Hatchery Breeds 26

   1) Layers 26

   2) Meat Breeds 27

   3) Dual Purpose 30

   4) Hybrids 32

   5) Show Breeds 33

Chapter 4: Choosing Your Chickens 36

   1) Space 36

Table of Contents

- 2) Purpose 36
- 3) How Many Chickens? 36
- 4) Location 37
- 5) Age 37

Chapter 5: Feeding 40
- 1) Digestive System 40
- 2) How and When to Feed 41
- 3) What to Feed 42
- 4) Do Not Feed 43
- 5) Treats 44

Chapter 6: Home Made Feed 48
- 1) How to Make Your Own Feed 48
- 2) Starter Feed 48
- 3) Grower Feed 50
- 4) Layer Feed 51

Chapter 7: Health 53
- 1) Vaccinations 53
- 2) Signs of Ill Health 53
- 3) Common Poisons 54
- 4) Injuries 55
- 5) Parasites 60
- 6) Common Diseases 62
- 7) Prevention of Disease 66
- 8) Hygiene 66
- 9) Keeping a Healthy Flock 68

Chapter 8: Housing 71
- 1) Coops 71

Table of Contents

    2) Runs 74

    3) Building Your Own Coop 75

    4) Feeders, Waterers and Dust Baths 75

    5) Foxes 76

Chapter 9: Care and Husbandry 78

    1) Handling Chickens 78

    2) Catching Chickens 79

    3) Carrying Chickens 80

    4) Stress and Chickens 81

Chapter 10: Hatching and Incubating 87

    1) Natural Hatching 87

    2) Artificial Hatching 91

    3) Brooders 98

    4) Raising Chicks 104

Chapter 11: Behavior 108

    1) Behaviors of a Happy Chicken 108

    2) Abnormal Behavior 111

    3) Mating Behavior 117

    4) Broodiness 118

Chapter 12: Eggs 119

    1) Collecting the Eggs 119

    2) Quality of Eggs 119

    3) Freshness 121

    4) Abnormalities in Eggs 122

    5) Egg Safety 124

    6) Nutritional Value of Eggs 125

    7) Problems in Egg Laying 126

Table of Contents

Chapter 13: Gardening With Chickens 131

   1) Chickens and Pests 131

   2) Dangerous Plants 132

   3) Vermin 132

Websites and Resources 133

Introduction

Introduction

Welcome to the world of chicken keeping. Chickens make fantastic pets. They are relatively low maintenance in comparison to other pets. They have individual personalities, some are social and affectionate, others can be more solitary and stand-offish. They can be easy to care for, provided you have all the necessary equipment and have someone willing to fill in for you if you are away. They can provide eggs and meat. The taste of a laid in your own backyard egg is indescribable compared to shop bought eggs. They can provide hours of entertainment and are useful in the garden. They are a pet for the whole family as children can be involved in the daily tasks of caring as well.

History of Chickens

Chickens are domesticated from the Red Junglefowl. They are scientifically classified as the same species and they can interbreed with the Red Junglefowl. They were originally domesticated for cockfighting and the benefits of egg and meat production were largely ignored. Aside from cockfighting, chickens were kept as clocks and for religious reasons.

The ancient Romans used them as oracles and omens. One belief was that a hen appearing from the left was a good omen. Another was that if caged 'sacred chickens' ate greedily when fed, then it was a good omen, if they stayed in the cage, flew away, beat their wings and made noises, then it was a bad omen. These chickens were looked after by pullarius, as the word for chicken was pulli, and fed pulses or a soft cake when an omen was needed. One Roman general, Publius Claudius Pulcher, had his chickens thrown overboard in 249 BC, because they refused to eat before a battle. He lost the battle with 93 ships sunk. He was tried for impiety, meaning he did not have piety, reverence and godliness

Introduction

for the chickens, and he was heavily fined.

Chickens have been, and still are, considered scared in many religions. In Hindu cremation ceremonies a chicken is tethered by the leg so as it is present for the ceremony. This is to ensure that any evil spirits which may also be present are transferred into the chicken and not the family members of the deceased. The chicken is then taken home and lives out the rest of its life. Roosters have been associated with the ancient Greek gods Ares and Hercules and the goddess Athena. The ancient Greeks believed that the lions were afraid of roosters and several of Aesop's Fables support this.

Christianity also has the rooster as a symbol. In the New Testament Jesus told Peter, a disciple, that Peter would betray him three times before the rooster crowed. The rooster became a Christian symbol for vigilance and betrayal. In the sixteenth century, Pope Gregory the First made the rooster an emblem of Christianity and in the ninth century Pope Nicholas ordered that every church steeple should have a figure of a rooster.

There are folk tales from central Europe, in which the devil is said to run away at the first morning crowing of a rooster. Myths also tell of a cockatrice. A cockatrice is a two legged dragon with a rooster's head. It was said to have hatched from an egg laid by a rooster and have the ability to turn people to stone, cause death by looking, touching or breathing. These powers did not diminish after the death of the cockatrice. It could be killed by making it look at itself, or by the crowing of a rooster. Weasels were the only animal immune to its powers.

In Judaism a kosher animal is swung around the head and slaughtered the afternoon before Yom Kippur. This practice is known as kapparos and the animal is usually a chicken or a fish as they are easy to handle and easily available. The animal takes on the sins of the person during kapparos and reminds people that the life of the person is in God's hands. The meat is donated to the poor. Women use a hen, while men use a rooster. The Talmud, a

Introduction

book of Judaism, also references the rooster. It says that men should learn courtesy towards their mate from the rooster. It also speaks of learning gallantry from cocks.

The chicken is also one of the Zodiac signs on the Chinese calendar. In the folk religions of the Chinese, cooked chicken is used as a religious offering but is only for the worship of village gods, or for honoring ancestors. It would not be offered to a vegetarian deity. In Confucian Chinese weddings, chickens can be used to substitute for a bride or groom who cannot attend due to serious illness or death. A red silk scarf is placed on the head of the chicken and a close relative of the missing person holds the bird. This practice is quite rare today.

By 162 BC, chickens had become a food source and books on recipes and breeding had been written. A Roman author Columella wrote a book offering advice on breeding chickens. The books also identifies Rhodic, Tangarian, Median and Chalkidic breeds which were used by the Greeks for cockfighting as they were quite aggressive. The Romans preferred native Roman breeds for farming or native females crossed with Greek roosters. Columella suggested that a flock of 200 birds was ideal and could be supervised by one person, with another watching for strays. He suggests that white chickens should be avoided as they are easily caught by eagles and not very fertile. He believed that the ratio should be one rooster to five hens unless the rooster was a heavy breed, in which case it should be one rooster to three hens.

He believed that heavy roosters were disinclined to mating. He believed that the hens of a heavy breed were not good mothers and would not incubate eggs properly so any eggs should be put under another breed. He also believed that long pointed eggs produced male chicks and rounded eggs produced more female chicks. Columella also stated that coops should face southeast and be close to the kitchen. The coop should have three rooms, a hearth and dust or ash for dust bathing. The chickens should be fed small chick peas, millet, barley groats and wheat bran, but not

Introduction

wheat itself. Boiled rye grass and the seeds and leaves of alfalfa can be given. Grape marc can be given with bran when egg production as ceased. Grape marc during egg laying produces small eggs and not very many of them. He said that parboiled barley increases fertility and should be mixed with alfalfa leaves, alfalfa seeds, or millet. Chickens should be slaughtered after three years of age.

It is probable that it was the Egyptians who began mass producing chickens and eggs as a source of food. It was in the mid 19th century that exhibition birds and breeding show birds became popular. This was largely due to Queen Victoria who was interested in chicken breeding and made it a popular hobby. There are several color variants of British breeds which were produced as a tribute to her.

Caging birds became popular after the Second World War. 93% of the United Kingdom national flock was caged. However, battery cages are now becoming less popular. Consumers are learning more about the conditions and lives of battery hens and are opposed to the welfare implications. At around one year of age, a battery hen's productivity declines and she is normally slaughtered. Battery birds are being rescued and are available for re-homing but they need a lot of attention and care to act like 'normal chickens. Free range and organic eggs are becoming more popular. Meat birds are also subject to intense farming. They are quickly fattened for slaughter and are usually ready at six weeks old. They are kept indoors in environmentally controlled environments.

They are given various medicines to prevent disease. The condition in the houses, however, contributes to illness and death. Many chickens die from heart failure due to the heat. The quick weight gain means that their legs are unable to support their bodies and this leads to various leg problems. The space constricts their movements. The ammonia in the air leads to respiration problems, eye problems and burns. Many people are more comfortable buying free range and organic chicken meat

Introduction

from farmers' markets and butchers as these birds can be traced back to their origins. Others prefer to raise their own chickens for meat and eggs, or for show.

Chickens also share genetic material with the Tyrannosaurus Rex dinosaur. They have similar bone structures and there have been discoveries of some feather like remains on dinosaur fossils. Scientists have examined dinosaur collagen, which is the main protein component of bone. These examinations have shown that the Tyrannosaurus Rex shares ancestry with chickens and ostriches. This supports the theory that dinosaurs evolved to become birds.

Chapter 1 : Life Stages

1) Roosters

Rooster is the term used for a male chicken in the United States, New Zealand, Australia and North America. Cockerel is the term used in the United Kingdom and Ireland. The word rooster was coined in 1772 as a puritan alternative to the word cock. Before this, the rooster was known as the roost cock, due to the perching or roosting behavior.

While hens have combs and wattles, those of a rooster are larger and more prominent. The color in the comb and wattle of a healthy rooster can be quite vibrant. The feathers of the tails, hackles and saddles tend to be longer. Rooster feathers are usually more brightly colored than hens.

A rooster will often sit on high perches and act as a lookout for the flock. He will guard the nest area and will crow if he thinks there are predators. He will also perch and crow to guard his territory against other roosters.

Roosters develop the crowing noise at around four months old along with developing hackles. While some hens may also crow, it is usually a noise attributed to only the males, and the males of all breed of chicken crow. They do not only crow at dawn. Some roosters will crow almost constantly while other will crow only a few times a day. The frequency of crowing can depend on the rooster's breed and his own individual personality. As well as the crowing, roosters have other noises. They can make a clucking noise which they will sometimes use to call their flock of hens to a food source. Some roosters will lead the hens to good nesting locations as well.

Roosters can be hand tamed like hens. However, some breeds are more aggressive and loud. These behaviors can be tamed by handling the bird. Despite this, some chicken owners advise not to keep a rooster around young children. Some breeds will be more docile and these may be fine around young children.

Roosters are not necessary for egg production. Hens are perfectly capable of producing eggs without a rooster. However, for eggs to hatch into chicks, then it is necessary for a rooster to fertilize the egg first.

2) Capons

Capons are castrated male chickens. The procedure is usually surgical and involves the removal of the testes, but there are methods of chemical caponization. This process is illegal in many parts of the world. After caponization, some of the typical male physical characteristics are changed. The hackle, tail and saddle feathers tend to grow much longer than a typical rooster's feathers would grow. The comb and wattle stop growing. Caponization takes place between three and five weeks of age.

Capons are considered a specialty meat item. Caponization slows the growth process which makes them gain more body fat. Capons are not as active as roosters. They are less aggressive and more docile. Rooster meat becomes coarse, tough and stringy as the rooster ages. Capon meat is tender, juicy and more flavorful than that of regular chicken.

3) Hens

A hen is the female chicken. Hens differ from roosters in that while they have combs and wattles, they are generally smaller and not as prominent. In many breeds, the feathers of a hen tend to be less colorful and shorter than a rooster's. In some breeds, such as the Sebright, the males and females are very similar in appearance.

A hen is the egg layer and does not need a rooster to do this. Any eggs laid without a rooster are unfertilized and cannot be incubated for hatching. Hens are a flock bird and, as such, need interaction with other birds to thrive. A flock of hens will have preferred nesting locations for the flock rather than a nest for each individual bird. Some hens will attempt to share a nest and incubation of the eggs. Shared nesting is dependent on the individual hen. Some hens prefer to nest alone but close to the flock, while others are more social and prefer to nest with other birds. Hens will lay until a clutch of eggs is complete. For most breeds a clutch is around twelve eggs. Once the clutch is complete, the hen will incubate the eggs until hatching. Some breeds of chicken make exceptional mothers and will rarely leave the nest during incubation. These breeds are also capable of hatching the eggs of other birds like ducks, who do not generally make good mothers. Once the chicks are several weeks old, the hen will begin to lay again.

4) Eggs

The development of an egg begins in the ovary of the hen as an oocyte, or egg yolk, during ovulation. It moves into the oviduct, where it can be fertilized by a sperm from a rooster, if there is one present in the flock. Each yolk contain a small white circle. This is actually a collection of cells which contain the genetic material of the hen. It is called a blastodisc in an unfertilized oocyte, and has an irregular shape. If it is fertilized, it becomes known as a blastoderm and has a regular bulls-eye pattern of circles. Regardless of whether or not fertilization occurred, the oocyte continues down the oviduct and is covered with a membrane called the vitelline membrane. It also becomes covered with layers of egg white, called albumin and other structural fibers. The part of the oviduct where this happens is called the magnus. The oviduct is a long spiral tube and as the egg travels through the oviduct, it rotates. The rotating movement of the egg twists the structural fibers to form rope like strands. This anchors the yolk in the egg white. These fibers are called chalazae and there are two to anchor each yolk on opposite ends. The egg shell is added around the egg in the lower part of the oviduct. Shells are

Chapter 1: Life Stages

made from a form of calcium carbonate called calcite. The entire process of egg development takes about a day.

5) Embryo Development

Assuming fertilization has taken place, the blastoderm, the circle of cells with the yolk, will develop into a chick. This development will begin once incubation starts. By day five of incubation, the nervous system, head, eyes, heart, ears, legs, wings, nose, and reproductive organs have begun to form. The heart begins to beat, and sex differentiation begins. The beak and egg tooth develop at day six, and the comb and feathers begin development at days seven and eight. By day nine, the embryo starts to look a little like a chick and its mouth opening develops. The beak begins to harden by day ten, and toes and tail feathers appear to be fully formed by days eleven and twelve. By day thirteen, the scales and claws begin to develop, and by day fifteen, the abdominal organs are drawn into the abdominal cavity. By day seventeen of incubation, feathers cover the body and the scales, claws and beak are firm. By day eighteen the growth and development of the embryo is very nearly complete. The yolk begins to be absorbed at around day nineteen. At days twenty and twenty one, the chick occupies most of the egg.

6) Chicks

A chick or a hatchling is a baby chicken. Chicks hatch out of the eggs after around 21 days of incubation. All chicks in the clutch generally hatch within a day or two of each other. The chick begin to make a peep noise inside the egg just before hatching. When the hen hears this she will cluck to encourage the chick to begin hatching. Hatching begins with a process called pipping. Pipping is when the chick uses its egg tooth to peck a breathing hole on the upper side of the blunt end of the egg. The chick will then rest for a few hours and absorb the remaining yolk and membrane. It will then enlarge the hole, eventually cracking the whole end of the egg. The chick is wet when it leaves the shell, but will dry as the hen will continue to nest for an extra two days after hatching.

Chapter 1: Life Stages

The chicks can survive on the absorbed nutrients from the egg yolk for about two days. After this the hen will lead them to food and water. She will also lead them to other edible treats, but it is rare for a hen to feed chicks directly. The hen is very protective and will nest with the chicks to keep them warm, rather than roost. After several weeks, the chicks are old enough to care for themselves.

7) Point of Lay

Point of lay birds are usually around 16 - 21 weeks old, depending on the breed. These are young hens which are just about to begin egg laying. They are on the point of laying. These birds are also known as pullets. Most hatcheries will have pullets available for purchase. When pullets arrive at their new home, it may take some time for them to settle in before they will begin to lay. Pullet eggs are generally smaller, but after a few months of laying, the pullet becomes a hen and the egg size increases. These birds should be fed a pullet feed and not layers feed, until they are at least eighteen weeks old. Then the feed can be gradually changed to a layers mix. There can be some dangers if a young bird is encouraged to begin laying too early. One of these can be a prolapse, where the oviduct protrudes out the vent.

Chapter 2: Anatomy

1) Parts of a Chicken

The external parts of a rooster and a hen are the same. This is part of why sexing chickens by looking at them is difficult until the males develop their combs and wattles. Roosters also have differently shaped tail and neck feathers and their color tends to be brighter and shinier. They also tend to be heavier than taller females of the same breed. While all chickens have the same parts, some breeds have five toes instead of four. The fifth toe always points to the back rather than forwards with the other four. Araucana chickens and Araucana crosses do not have tail feathers. The reasons behind this is unclear but it is due to selective breeding.

Starting at the head of the chicken, the comb comes first. The comb may be one of several shapes but the purpose remains the same. It acts as a cooling device for the bird. Small combs were bred for cold weather climates. Large combs are more useful in warm weather climates as they can cool the bird better but are prone to frostbite in cold weather and may fall off.

The eyes are small and yellow with gray, black or brown pupils. They are on the sides of the head. This placement gives them a wide field of vision meaning they can detect predators from almost every angle. Chickens do have eyelids. Chickens are not color blind and can see in color. Chickens sleep with the eyes closed. They recognize chickens that they already know by the facial features, but the need to be within twenty four inches of each other to do this.

The ears of a chicken are just very small openings on the side of

Chapter 2: Anatomy

the head. These openings are often covered by feathers. The ear is surrounded by red or white bare skin. While feathers may cover this, no feathers grow in this area. The skin color of this area can indicate the color of the eggs. Red skin here usually means that the bird will lay brown eggs. White skin generally means that the bird will lay white eggs. The exceptions are Easter Eggers, the Araucana and the Ameraucana. These breeds have red skin but lay greenish blue eggs. There can be a fleshy ear lobe hanging from the bottom of the skin patch. In most breeds the ear lobe is red, but in some breeds it is blue or black.

The beak of a chicken is made of an upper half and a lower half. The lower half slots into the upper half perfectly. There should not be a gap between the two halves when the beak is closed. Both halves of the beak should be straight and not twisted. The beak is made from a horn like material and is used to pick up food and for grooming. The color of the beak is dependent on the breed of the chicken. Some breeds have yellowish beaks while other breeds can have dark blue or gray beaks. All chickens are born with beaks and to aid in hatching, the beaks of chicks have a thickened part which is known as the egg tooth. It is not a true tooth and chickens do not have teeth. The tongue is triangle shaped and has barbs which push the food to the back of the mouth and down the throat. Chickens have around 20 - 30 taste buds. Humans have over 10,000. The chicken's sense of taste is very limited in comparison.

Their sense of smell, however is around the same as a human sense of smell. The nostrils or nares of a chicken are surrounded by the cere, which is a raised tan patch. The nostrils should be clean and open. Large combs can come down and partially hide the nostrils.

The wattles are the fleshy lobes coming from under the beak on each side. They can be large or small depending on the breed. The can be red, maroon, black, or other colors and again this depends on the breed. The wattles of a rooster are more prominent than those of a hen.

Chapter 2: Anatomy

The neck of a chicken should be slender and quite long. It is covered with small downward pointing feathers known as the hackle feathers. The neck is designed to allow the birds to look over tall grasses and shrubs for predators.

The body is u-shaped in that the neck and tail come higher than the back. The breast is the plump flesh under the neck. In meat breeds this will be more pronounced that in laying breeds. As birds do not feed their young like mammals, they do not have or have no need of mammary glands which produce milk in mammals.

The back between the neck and tail is called the saddle. The saddle feathers in roosters tend to be bold, vibrant and colorful. Some chicken owners protect this area from injury by putting a saddle made from durable materials on. This can protect a hen from a rooster who mates aggressively and can protect less dominant birds from aggressive feather pecking of more dominant birds. However, if feather pecking is happening in the flock, it needs to be investigated as there will be a reason for this.

The wings come from each side of the body, just below the neck. They have a joint in the middle and the bones in the wing are hollow. Chickens are not considered a bird of flight but they do have all the things necessary for flight like wings, hollow bones and other internal systems to keep body weight light. They will fly short distances if they think they are in danger.

The tail feathers are long and usually curved but the curve and length can vary depending on the breed. Some breeds of chicken may have no tail feathers at all. The tails of roosters are brightly colored and shiny. There is no function to the tail of domesticated chickens other than aesthetic appeal. The tails of hens are much smaller and are not as colorful.

The legs of a chicken are covered in scales. The roosters will have a spur which is a bony, hard protrusion at the back of the leg. In roosters, the spur can be large and in hens, if they have a spur at

Chapter 2: Anatomy

all, it will be small. The spur does not touch the ground. Most breeds of chicken have four toes which are forward facing but some breeds may have a fifth toe at the back of the foot which points backwards. The males will use their toes and spurs to fight other males. As the chicken matures the scales of the leg can become rougher. The legs are usually yellow but some breeds can have black, white or gray legs.

The skin of a chicken is usually white or yellow in color. The exception to this is the Silkie which has black skin. The skin color is influenced by diet. Free range chickens and birds who are fed a lot of corn take on a darker tone to yellow skin and the white skin takes on a creamy color. There are follicles over the skin which is where the feathers grow. The flesh is loose and can tear easily.

2) Feathers

Most breeds of chicken have feathers covering all of the body but there are some breeds which have been bred to have an area bare or un-feathered, such as the Turken, which has no feathers on the neck. Chickens who have sleek and shiny feathers are said to be hard feathered, while birds who have fluffy and loose feathers are said to be soft feathered. The feathers which cover the ear lobes in some breeds are called muffs. Other breeds have feathers hanging down under the beak which are known as beards. Some breeds have a covering of feathers on the leg and some breeds have this covering down to the toes. Some breeds have a crest or a topknot which is a large tuft of feather on the top of the head which can be large enough to come down and cover the eyes and partially cover the nostrils in some breeds. Some feathers have a mutation which causes them to curl and stick out randomly. Birds with this mutation are sometimes know as frizzles. The feathers are molted and regrown.

The outer feathers which form the shape of the wings, tail, and body are known as the contour feathers. The contour feathers have a strong shaft in the middle of the feather and barbs. It is these that give the feather a strong shape. The insulating layer of

Chapter 2: Anatomy

feathers close to the body are the down feathers. Down feathers do not have barbs. The feathers of Silkies don't have barbs either and this gives them the fluffy appearance.

Feathers are made from keratin, which is the same substance as human fingernails and hair are made from. There is a central shaft which attaches the feather to the skin of the bird. There are follicles on the skin where the feather grows and there are muscles which move the feathers. It is these muscles that the bird uses to fluff up the feathers. The bottom of a mature feather shaft is hollow and is called a quill. The shaft of an immature feather has a vein running inside it. This will bleed if the feather is cut or torn. The maturity of the feather is not related to the maturity of the bird. Immature feathers are also known as pin-feathers. This is because as they begin to grow they are tightly rolled and appear like pins coming from the skin. Immature feathers have a white coating which is groomed off by the bird or gradually wears off. Once this covering is removed the feather will expand. Once the feather has grown to the full length, the vein in the shaft will dry up. There are barbs on either side of the shaft. Each barb has barbules. These have hooks along the edge. These hooks lock on to the other barbules which creates a smooth feather. When a chicken grooms and preens itself, they are smoothing and locking the barbules together again.

While there are contour and down feathers, their location on the body is important. The area of the bird that the feathers are on also changes the terminology and function of the feather.

The feathers making the row of feathers on the neck of the bird are called hackles. Hackles on a rooster are often very colorful, bold and vibrant. In many breeds the hackle feathers of the rooster are pointed and shiny. The hackles of a hen are more rounded in shape and duller in color and shine. Hackles can stand up to signify anger.

The feathers on the under side of a chicken are small and fluffy. In many breeds, these feathers will be a lighter color than the color of the main body. There are also feathers on the thighs. These feathers are also small and soft. In many chicken breeds the feathers on the leg stop at the leg joint, but in some breeds the feathers cover the leg. In other breeds the leg feathers cover the legs and go down to the end of the toes.

The tail feathers are known as sickle feathers. In a rooster these feathers are long, shiny and colorful. The top three or four tail feathers may arch over the rest of the tail feathers and they are slightly narrower than the others. The tail feathers of the hen are not as colorful. They may have a fan shape. They are shorter than the tail feathers of the rooster as well.

3) Markings

As there are many different breeds of chicken, there are many colors and many markings. Different breeds come in different colors, but each breed also has different markings. There is different terminology associated with each marking.

Barring - barring is used to describe the stripes of light and dark coloring across each feather.
Cuckoo banding - this is used when the stripes have indistinct boundaries.
Double laced - this is when there are two stripes around the edges of each feather.
Frizzled - this is used to describe feathers which curl backwards so that the tip of the feathers points to the head.
Lacing - this is a single thin stripe around the edges of the feather.
Moons - this is used to describe circular spangles at the tips of the feathers.
Mossy - this is a muddled marking.
Mottled - this is when the feathers have spots of different color.
Pencilling - this is fine lines on the feathers.
Peppering - this is when there small dots of a darker color over a lighter color.
Spangled - this is when there is a spot of a different color on the ends of the feathers.

Chapter 2: Anatomy

Splashed - this is when a contrasting color to the ground color is splashed randomly on the feathers.
Ticked - this is when the feathers have a v shaped marking on the tip.
Wing bar - this is a line of color across the middle of the wing..

Other marking and color terminology:

Bay - this is used to describe a brown red color.
Brassiness - this is used for a yellow color on the back and wings.
Dusky - this is a yellow black color.
Foxy - this is a rusty red color.
Gay - this is used to describe plumage with too much white marking.
Ground Color - this is used for the main color of the plumage.
Lustre - this is used to describe shiny plumage unless the main color is black.
Mealy - this is used when the ground color is mottled with a lighter color.
Nankin - this is a yellowy color. The term is derived from nankeen cloth.
Self Color - this is used when the color is uniform.
Sheen - this is the green shine on black feathers. In other colors, it is lustre.
Under Color - This is the color of the fluffier feathers under the main feathers.

4) Combs

There are several different types of comb. All chickens have combs, but a rooster's comb is usually more prominent than a hen's. Combs, like wattles, are used for temperature regulation. They are also a good way to gauge health. A pale comb can be an indicator that there is something wrong. A good red color is also a sign that the chicken is ready to mate and a large comb on a rooster is used to attract mates. There are different shapes of comb. Some of these have been selectively bred to enhance the look of the comb. The biggest risk to the comb is cold weather. It

Chapter 2: Anatomy

is possible to remove the comb, wattles and ear lobes through a process known as dubbing. This would usually happen at six months old and is most often only used for male chickens. The comb, wattle and ear lobes won't grow back.

The Single
This is the most common type of comb. It is a straight row of spikes beginning at the nostril and going back (?? down) the head. It has three sections, the front, the middle, and the end which is known as the blade. It is possible for combs to get frostbite and this can cause the points or spikes to fall off. While this does not usually cause any health problems, it does affect the value as an exhibition bird. It can be a good idea to cover the comb with petroleum jelly. This insulates the comb and prevents frostbite. This can be done for show birds and pets.

The Pea
Pea combs usually have three rows of bumps alongside each other. These bumps, called peas, are usually incredibly similar in size and shape. However, as the bird grows, some pea combs can lose their shape and appearance.

The Rose
A rose comb is flat and close to the head. It can extend further back than the rest of the comb forming a point. The shape differs depending on the breed, but the top should be a little raised and has small round bumps.

The Buttercup
This comb consists of a small single comb in the middle with larger ones on both sides.

The Strawberry
The strawberry comb is similar to a rose comb, but has no point and is raised higher. These combs resemble strawberries.

The Cushion
This comb is also similar to the rose comb, but it is more rounded

in appearance and smaller. It has no point and should be smooth with no bumps or hollows.

The Walnut
This comb resembles the shape and appearance of a walnut. It is round, large and pitted. They can grow to huge sizes.

The V
The V comb is two hornlike points which are joined at the base.

The Carnation
This comb is quite rare. It consists of a single comb with side sprigs on either side at the back of the comb.

Chapter 3: The Hatchery Breeds

Chapter 3: The Hatchery Breeds

1) Layers

Breeds meant purely for egg laying tend to be of a small size. They mature earlier than other classes of chickens. They usually lay an egg every day or two. Layers are usually of a more active and nervous temperament and they rarely go 'broody', and those that do often stop before incubation is complete. This means that they can have longer periods of egg production without interruption. They are good, active foragers. Layer birds tend to be more sensitive to cold. They need sunlight or artificial light for egg production and they will stop laying during their molting. Some of the best layer breeds originate in the Mediterranean such as the Leghorn, the Minorca, the White-faced Black Spanish, and the Andalusian. However, because the layer class does not go broody as often as other classes, it can be difficult to breed from these birds as a beginner chicken keeper.

Leghorn
The Leghorn originated in Tuscany, Italy. They were initially called Italians. The name Leghorn derives from Livorno, which is the Tuscan port city from which they were first exported. The breed was first accepted as having three color variations - white, black and brown of both light and dark shades. However, now there are more color variants accepted, although the poultry associations of different countries accept varying numbers of color variant. For example, the French poultry federation, Fédération Française de Volailles, divides the breed into four types and lists seventeen color variants for full size modern type Leghorns, and fourteen for bantams of the modern type. The current conservation status of this breed is recovering.

Chapter 3: The Hatchery Breeds

In terms of egg laying, Leghorns lay an average of 280 white eggs per year. They are a light breed, who tend to be nervous around humans.

The Minorca
The Minorca originated in Spain. They are closely related to the White-Faced Black Spanish and the Castillian Black. They are the largest of the Mediterranean breeds, but are similar in that they rarely show broodiness and are flighty and nervous around humans. They can be tamed if regularly handled as chicks. They have a large white ear patch and a large comb. They are sensitive to cold and can suffer from comb frostbite if in cold climates. They lay white eggs

The White-Faced Black Spanish
The White-faced Black Spanish originated in Spain, and is thought to be the oldest Mediterranean chicken. They have black glossy plumage and overdeveloped, white, low hanging ear lobes. They lay around 150 - 180 large white eggs per year. They do not show broodiness. They have a single comb and four toes. They have been nicknamed Clown chickens and The Fowls of Seville.

The Andalusian
The Andalusian originated in Andalusia, Spain. The only color pattern recognized is blue and because of this they are often called Blue Andalusians. However, when breeding two blue Andalusians, the chicks may be blue, black or a white color known as splash. The difficulties in breeding mean that they are quite rare other than among breed enthusiasts. They are active and lay white eggs. They are graceful, and compact.

2) Meat Breeds

Breeds intended purely for meat are larger in size. They are less nervous and of a gentle temperament. They tend to be slow moving and are not active foragers. They are generally poor layers, but are often broody. They tend to mature late and they generally do not wander or fly off. Some of the best meat breeds

Chapter 3: The Hatchery Breeds

are Brahmas, Cochins, and Langshans, all of which are Asiatic. Another good meat breed is the Jersey Giant, which originated from the United States. Modern meat breeds are usually hybrids.

Brahmas
There are two theories as to the origin of the Brahma. The first is that they were developed in the United States from a breed imported from China. The imported chickens came from Shanghai and became known as Shanghai birds. It is thought that cross breeding the large Shanghai birds with Chittagong chickens from Bangladesh led to the Brahma, which gave them their head shape and pea comb. The second origin theory of the Brahma is that they originated in India near the Brahma Putra River. The Brahma is a large meat breed, which was very popular from around 1850 - 1930. They are tall when standing, with strong feet and feather legs. They are closely feathered. The American Standard of Perfection recognizes three color variants - Light Dark and Buff. However, the Australian Poultry Association accepts black, blue, partridge, barred and crele variants as well. They lay brown eggs and in addition to being a meat breed, they are a good winter layer.

Cochin
The Cochin was developed in the United States from the Shanghai birds. They were bred entirely based on their aesthetic appearance. They are large with fluffy feathers and feathered legs and feet. There are eighteen accepted color variants. They are broody, and slow maturing. They lay brown eggs. They are friendly, quiet and calm birds, which makes them ideal pets. The full size Cochin is classed as Asiatic but the bantam variety is classed as Feather Legged. The bantam Cochin is often called a Pekin Bantam, but it is not actually the Pekin Bantam.

Jersey Giant
Jersey Giants originated in New Jersey. They were developed as a replacement bird for the turkey and were used as a meat breed. They were produced by crossing Black Java, Black Langshan and Dark Brahma chickens. The Black Jersey Giant was officially

declared as a breed in 1922 by the American Standard of perfection. White Jersey Giants were declared as a breed in 1947. The Black Jersey Giant tends to be around a pound heavier than the White Jersey Giant. Present day Jersey Giants are not as large as past Jersey Giants. They are slow to mature. The current conservation status is 'watch.' They were almost extinct before a UK breeder tried to revive the breed in the 1980's. He built up a flock but inbreeding became an issue. A Dutch chicken breeder had tried to do the same thing in the Netherlands and so the two breeders could share stock, eliminate the problems of inbreeding and they re-introduced the Jersey Giant to both countries. They are a calm, docile breed but are slow growers. They are quite robust and are not overly sensitive to the cold. Color variants now include Blue, as well as Black and White. They do not have feathered legs and have a single comb. They lay brown eggs.

Langshan
The Langshan has four varieties - The Croad, the German, the Australian, and the Modern.

The Croad Langshan
The Croad Langshan probably originated in China. It is an old, heavy meat breed. The first record of importing comes from the Langshan district in 1872 when Major F.T. Croad imported the breed to Britain and his niece established the breed. Numbers of this breed declined after the Second World War. It was imported to America in 1878 and there are three accepted color variations-Black, White and Blue. Although the three color variants are accepted, the main one is black with a green sheen. They are large bodied with a small head. They have a single comb and are slightly feathered. They lay dark brown eggs. They are docile and easily tamed. They thrive both indoors and free range in sheltered conditions.

The German Langshan
The German Langshan was developed from the Croad Langshan. It is a large, tall and robust breed. Standard size German Langshan are quite rare in the United Kingdom and the United

States, but the bantam size is popular in the UK. They are fast growing and because of their size and weight, do not fly. They are easily tamed and docile. They have a single comb and lay large cream eggs. They are generally Black, Blue and White. Other colors have been known but are rare.

The Australian Langshan

The Australian Langshan was developed in Australia from Croad Langshans crossed with other breeds. They are popular within Australia but have not gained favor outside it. They are in standard and bantam size with three color variants - Black, Blue and White. They have a single comb and lay brown eggs

The Modern Langshan

The Modern Langshan was derived from the Croad Langshan and was once very popular. It was bred to have longer, lightly feathered legs, closer feathers and a less heavy build. It has a single comb and lays brown eggs.

3) Dual Purpose

Dual purpose breeds are bred to be both egg layer and meat birds, although some breeds can be better for one more than the other. They are medium sized birds and tend to be more active than meat breeds but less active than layer breeds. They are good incubators and mothers. They are usually good table birds and good layers. Some of the best dual purpose breeds include Plymouth Rocks, Wyandottes, Rhode Island Reds and the Sussex.

Plymouth Rock

The Plymouth Rock originated in the United States as dual purpose birds. They are often called Rocks or Barred Rocks, due to the most popular color. They are hardy in the cold, docile and broody, which makes them an excellent bird for small farm and back yard chicken keepers. The first Plymouth Rocks were of the Barred color variant, but other varieties have developed. The Barred Plymouth Rock was one of the foundation stock breeds for the broiler industry and the White Plymouth Rock is still used as

Chapter 3: The Hatchery Breeds

the female in the production of broiler stock. Some strains are better for egg production while others are a better meat breed. There are eight variants in the UK and USA, while Australia has nine. The eggs are large and range in color from light to medium brown with a little pink. They are good layers and lay in winter but with decreased egg production. They are broody and are good mothers. They have a single comb.

Wyandotte
Wyandottes originated in the United States as a dual purpose breed. They are of medium size and have a rose comb. They are docile and calm. There are seventeen color variants with eight recognized by the American Poultry Association. Other colors are accepted by similar organizations in other countries. The feathers are particularly fluffy around the vent which makes insemination challenging. This also means that feces can stick to these feathers and will need to be cleaned or the vent may become clogged. They lay around 200 eggs per year and the egg color ranges from light brown to tan. They are broody and make good mothers. The color variants should not be inter-bred.

Rhode Island Reds
The Rhode Island Red is a dual purpose bird which originates in the United States. They are great egg layers. Dependent on care and condition, they can lay 5-7 eggs per week. They are a popular breed for backyard flocks as they are a hardy breed. They lay brown eggs and have a single comb. The feathers are a rust color, however darker reds have been known. They have red-orange eyes and reddish-brown beaks. They are used in cross breeding for hybrid birds.

Sussex
The Sussex is a dual purpose chicken, originating in England. They are a very popular breed for backyard chicken breeders as they are docile and hardy. They are adaptable to most conditions and can live well indoors or free range, although for mating and breeding they do better in larger spaces. They are active, and good foragers. They are easily tamed. They lay 240 - 260 eggs per year.

The eggs range from cream to light brown in color. They are broody and good mothers. There are eight color variants in the standard size and eight color variants in the bantam size. They are also a good meat bird. They mature slowly for a heavy breed. The speckled variant is the slowest to mature but all varieties make a good table bird.

4) Hybrids

Hybrids are bred for a specific purpose. They are cross bred from pure bred breeds. They are similar to dual purpose breeds in that they are both good layer and good table birds. They are usually cheaper to buy than pure bred birds. They have no conservation or show value as they are the result of cross breeding, unlike dual purpose breeds which do have conservation value. Most hatcheries will have hybrids available. Hybrid breeds include the Daisy Belle, the White Star, The Freedom Ranger. The speckled Humbug, The Rhode Island Ranger and the Bluebell.

The Daisy Belle
The Daisy Belle is a hybrid bird developed by crossing the Rhode Island Red and the Sussex. They are large and are more suited to free range environments rather than indoor ones. They lay around 240 - 300 eggs per year. The eggs are brown in color. They have black bodies with a silver white neck and head.

The White Star
The White Star is a smallish white bird. They are developed from Leghorns and can lay around 320 eggs per year. They can be nervous of humans and flighty. The eggs are large and white in color.

The Freedom Ranger
The Freedom Ranger was developed in France to meet the standards of the quality assurance program for food and as an alternative to the Cornish Cross. They are better suited to a free range environment. They are slow growing but as they thrive better as a free range bird. They are considered by some to be a

Chapter 3: The Hatchery Breeds

more nutritious and tastier chicken.

The Speckled Humbug
The Speckled Humbug is based on the German Maran. They lay around 280 eggs per year. The eggs are medium to dark brown in color. The feathers are dark gray with a barred pattern. They are friendly and docile birds.

The Rhode Island Ranger
The Rhode Island Ranger is a hybrid of the Rhode Island Red. It is a friendly bird and generally enjoys handling, making it ideal as a children's pet. It is chestnut in color and lays around 300 eggs per year. The eggs are medium brown in color.

The Bluebell
The Bluebell is a hybrid developed from the Rhode Island Red and the Maran. They are friendly birds and have a good nature. They are blue gray in color. They lay around 240 brown eggs per year.

5) Show Breeds

Show breeds include various kinds of Bantam, Poland and Silkies. Show breeds are bred for aesthetics and generally do not have a purpose beyond that. However, some breeds which are now show breeds were originally bred for cockfighting. The breeds which were cockfighting breeds are exhibited as Game Fowl.

American Game Bantam
The American Game Bantam is a show breed. It is recognized by the ABA but it is not recognized by the APA. These chickens are ideal for beginners. They are good layers and are excellent mothers. They have a single comb and a variety of colors are accepted including white, and blue. They originate from New Jersey and are a good breed for chicken owners who would like to start showing birds.

Chapter 3: The Hatchery Breeds

Dutch Bantam

The Dutch Bantam originated in Holland. There are no large varieties of this breed and it is the smallest recognized bantam. It is quite a popular show breed. This breed can fly quite well and therefore they need good fencing. This breed does not do well in cold climates and needs to be sheltered very well. They are good mothers and will lay well during spring, summer and fall. There are no feathers on the legs and they have a single comb. There are several color varieties accepted such as black, silver, cuckoo and golden.

Japanese Bantam

The Japanese Bantam originates from Japan, although it is believed that they arrived from China in the early 1600s. There is no large variety of the Japanese Bantam. They are a popular breed that is not suitable for beginners. It can be hard to breed them to show standard. They must be kept on clean, dry bedding. This breed can only go outside in dry weather. They may need an additional heat source in the coop during winter or cold weather. The hens are relatively good layers and they make excellent mothers. They have a single comb and clean legs. There are several accepted color varieties including black, buff, gray and wheaten.

Manx Rumpy

The Manx Rumpy is a breed of chicken which has no skeletal tail structure. Originally these birds were known as Persian Rumpless but, at some point became known as Manx Rumpy because of the resemblance to the Manx cat. They are very good free range birds. They are good egg layers but the fertility is quite low, which can make them quite hard to breed. They originate from Persia. They feed almost exclusively from foraging outside, although some feed may need to be provided.

Modern Game

The Modern Game is a show breed which was never actually used as a fighting bird. This breed has been developed from fighting birds, and because of this they can be aggressive. They are slow

Chapter 3: The Hatchery Breeds

to mature and they do not thrive in cold. They have a single comb and a variety of color variations are accepted. There are both standard and bantam varieties. They make good mothers and can lay a fair amount of eggs.

Chapter 4: Choosing Your Chickens

1) Space

The first thing that needs to be considered before getting your chickens is the space available. If you have a limited space available then perhaps a bantam version would be more appropriate. Bantams eat less than standard size birds and lay smaller eggs. Silkies also do well in a smaller area. They are also a good breed with children. They have a good temperament. Some breeds require more space than others, and some do not do well in an indoor environment. The housing space available should also be considered.

2) Purpose

The purpose of the chickens also needs to be thought about. Ornamental birds such as Silkies are appealing as they make wonderful pets. They are broody and make good mothers. They are not excellent egg layers. They lay around 80 - 100 eggs per year. Egg laying hybrids would be a good choice if egg production is a factor in the choice of breed. They are cheaper than the pure bred breeds. Pure bred egg layers can also be found at a hatchery. Pure bred birds tend to be hardier and less susceptible to disease and illness. A rule of thumb is to allow two egg laying hens for each person of the household. However if space is limited, this may not be possible, meaning that a breed with a higher egg production rate may be the best choice.

3) How Many Chickens?

The exact number of chickens will depend on the available space and the breed. However, chickens are social animals so it is better to have two or more chickens. They are a flock bird. Keeping a rooster in your flock will depend on how much space is available for them. If there is limited space, it is best to keep only one rooster. If there is more space, then two roosters could live together with the space to stay out of each other's way. A single rooster can fertilize 10 - 15 hens. However, some areas, particularly urban and suburban areas, do not allow roosters to be kept as pets. It is a good idea to check the laws in your area before getting a rooster. As well as fertilizing the eggs, roosters are also very noisy. The will make a loud crowing sound when they feel threatened, and to mark their territory. If there are two or more roosters in a small space, they will fight. Roosters can leave each other badly injured and bleeding after a fight. They will use talons and beaks to cause as much damage as possible.

Hens do not fight when in groups. They form a pecking order, that is, they arrange themselves into order from most dominant to least dominant. The dominant bird in the flock has priority access to food, water and her choice of nesting location. Once this pecking order has been established, it tends not to change unless new birds are introduced. After new birds have been introduced to an established flock, the pecking order may change to include them. Hens do not tend to be as aggressive when arranging the pecking order as roosters are when fighting. Any injury sustained is liable to be very minor.

4) Location

The location is also important. Some breeds do not do well in cold weather. If you are in an area prone to cold weather, then breeds which suffer from comb frostbite would not be suitable. The soil type can also be a factor but it is not as important as the weather conditions.

5) Age

The hatchery will be able to help you choose the best breed for your needs and circumstances and they will have a selection of ages available. There will usually be chicks, point of lay or adult

Chapter 4: Choosing Your Chickens

birds.

Chicks
Chicks are much easier to handle. They are small and cute and will probably be handled frequently. This means that there will be a greater chance for bonding. They are unlikely to carry disease or infection. They will probably be cheaper to purchase than older birds. Sexed chicks, meaning that they have not been sorted into gender, are usually more expensive than unsexed chicks. This also means that you can choose how many males and females you want. It is highly probable that female sexed chicks will cost more than unsexed or male chicks. Many of the hybrid breeds can be sexed by the color of the down or the length of the wing feather. This is called auto-sexing, but it is not an exact science. Unsexed chicks are cheaper than sexed chicks.

However, when buying unsexed chicks, you may end up with more roosters than expected. Chicks will need to be fed and housed for around 20 weeks before they will begin egg laying. They will also need a warm house or box known as a brooder. The brooder will help keep them warm and should be small enough to keep them close together.

Point of Lay Pullets
Point of lay birds are around 20 weeks old at the time of purchase. Buying point of lay birds is the quickest way to start getting eggs. Pullets usually start laying two to six weeks after purchase. You should ask how the birds have been reared and if the hatchery has advice on the future management, such as the feeding schedule, the type of food and lighting regime.

Adult Birds
Adult birds are usually around 18 months and are considered to be past their usefulness. Adult birds are, most often, ex-battery birds. They may be getting ready to molt, after which they will lay bigger but fewer eggs. These birds may have lost feather through the stress of their previous environment. It can take a lot of time and patience for an ex-battery chicken to behave in a more

Chapter 4: Choosing Your Chickens

normal way. Some of the abnormal behaviors battery birds exhibit may never fully cease but can be reduced. They can be frightened of having more space than before, although when given proper care, attention and supervision, they can flourish into great pets.

Chapter 5: Feeding

1) Digestive System

Chickens use their beaks to peck and take in bits of food. Some digestive enzymes and saliva are added to the food as it moves from the mouth into the esophagus. The esophagus connects to the crop. The crop is a storage area for the food. It is expandable and can store the food for up to twelve hours. The food then moves into the stomach. The stomach of a chicken has two parts. The first part is the proventriculus. The proventriculus has also been referred to as the true stomach. This is where a lot of the digestive enzymes and stomach acids are added to the food. The food then passes to the gizzard or ventriculus.

This second part of the stomach is a muscular organ which does what teeth would do. It grinds the food and helps mix it with digestive enzymes. Chicken regularly eat grit and small stones and these are stored in the gizzard. It is these stones and grit which aid in the grinding process. The food then passes through the pancreas and liver. Both the pancreas and the liver aid in breaking the food down further. The intestines help digest the food and also absorb nutrients from it.

Chickens have two ceca. Ceca are pouches located at the join of the large and small intestines. The ceca absorb extra nutrients, particularly fatty acids and B vitamins, as the fermentation process occurs there. The ceca empty a froth which can be a mustard color and has a foul odor. This is sometimes confused with diarrhea. The kidneys of a chicken are not used to produce urine as in mammals. Instead they produces urates which are the urinary system waste of a bird. The kidneys filter the waste product from the blood and pass it through the ureters to the

Chapter 5: Feeding

cloaca. It is mixed with darker colored undigested materials. This mixture is passed to the outside through the vent.

2) How and When to Feed

Chicken feed must be placed in a feeder, slightly raised from the ground. This is to keep the food clean. Only buy a feeder which will hold enough food for your flock. Chickens do not over eat and excess food will get stale if the feeder is too big. Feeders do not have to be in the chicken house, but if it is necessary, they should be hung rather than on the floor. The feeder should be hanging at around the height of the chicken's neck. This is to prevent vermin from accessing your chicken food.

The amount to feed depends on a number of factors: the season, the temperature, the age of the bird, the size of the bird, the weight of the bird, and how much the bird lays. Chickens will usually only eat enough food to meet their energy needs, so the amount of energy in the feed is also a factor. As they will use more energy in cold weather to keep warm, they will eat more in cold weather. If they do not eat enough to meet their energy needs, they will not thrive or lay well. Some chickens will under eat when molting. The chickens on the lower end of the pecking order may not get as much as they need. Some chickens won't eat enough just because they don't like the food. They can be fussy about the texture of the food, and don't like food that has a dusty or powdery residue. If the chickens are under-eating, supplementing the food with treats can encourage them to eat more.

Overeating can be a sign of worms in chickens. A vet can analyze a sample of feces for this and provide a medicine to worm the chickens. Chickens will also eat more in winter, so it can be advisable to increase the carbohydrate intake to help meet their energy needs. It should also be considered that a disappearance of food may not be entirely due to the chickens. Chickens attract pests such as mice and rats and other birds may also be eating from the chicken feeder.

Chapter 5: Feeding

There are two methods of feeding chickens. Free choice or 'ad lib feeding' means that the chickens always have access to the food. They can eat when they want and need to. The benefit to this is that the feeders will not need to be refilled as often and that a chicken who is on the lower end of the pecking order is unlikely to under eat. It is more likely that she will wait until the more dominant birds have eaten and will then have her turn. The drawbacks to this method are that the food is also freely available for other birds and pests. It will be harder to observe how much each bird eats, so it will be difficult to tell if a bird is under eating. It can be more difficult to handle and tame birds which are fed ad lib.

The second method of feeding is restricted feeding. This means that a certain amount of feed is provided at a certain time. This method allows more chance to interact with the chickens, and observe how much each bird is eating, although, it is worth noting that some chicken owners and breeders believe that this method can lead to cannibalism.

Clean water should always be available. Water should be replaced every two to three days as it can be contaminated or have algae develop. A hen will drink around 240ml or 8 fluid ounces of water per day, but this will increase in hot weather.

3) What to Feed

There are several brands of complete feeds available for purchase. There are also several types of feed available. The type you choose will depend on the age of the birds and their purpose. Chicks should be fed a chick crumb feed until 6-8 weeks old. About a week before the switch over to feed for older chicks, it is advisable to mix the chick crumb and the new feed together so as to gradually change the feed. Feeds can come in pellet or mash form. The choice is up to you and your chickens. Some chicken owners prefer pellets as there is less mess and their chickens prefer the pellets. There is also feed designed specifically for meat birds and feeds for layers. It is not a good idea to start pullets on a

Chapter 5: Feeding

layers mix at first. It may encourage them to lay early and this can cause problems. Your local feed merchant will be able to advise you as to the best mix for your birds based on what is available in your area. The choice of brand can depend on what your budget is or individual preference. Also your chickens may prefer one brand over another. It is also possible to mix your own feed, but it is time consuming and you may need to supplement the feed to make sure that all the nutritional needs are being met. It is far easier to buy a ready mixed commercial feed.

Other supplements may be needed. Hens require grit, and something like oyster shell can help with good egg shell formation and provide calcium.

4) Do Not Feed

There are some foods which are harmful to chickens for various reasons. These foods should never be fed to your chickens:

Salty foods - Chickens are not capable of eating large amounts of salt. Too much salt in the diet can cause hypernatremia, or salt poisoning.

Plants from the Nightshade family - There are toxins in the leaves, flesh and peels of raw, uncooked Nightshade plants. The Nightshade family includes tomatoes, eggplants and potatoes. Some people say that cooked potato is fine to feed occasionally.

Citrus - Some breeds of chicken are sensitive to citrus. It can cause feather plucking behavior.

Onions - Onions contain a toxin called thiosulphate. This toxin destroys red blood cells. This can cause jaundice and anemia. It can be fatal.

Dry rice - Dry rice should never be fed to your chickens. Once dry rice reaches the stomach, it is introduced to moisture and can puff up, which could cause problems in the gut. Chickens can eat cooked rice.

Sugar - Chocolate, particularly, has a toxin called methylxanthines theobromine. This can effect the digestive tract.

Dry beans - Dry or under-cooked beans have a toxin called hemaglutin which is toxic to chickens.

Apple seeds - Apple seeds have traces of arsenic. The apple flesh is fine to be fed on occasion.

Avocado skins and pits - Chickens tend not to like these anyway, but the skin and pit of avocados have low levels of toxicity.

5) Treats

Chickens can be given treats on occasion. Each chicken will more than likely have a preference as to which treat she prefers. Some treats have little to no nutritional value. Also, chickens may not always know what is good for them and what is not, so it is always advisable to watch to ensure they are not eating foods that could be harmful for them. Vegetable treats should not be fed on the floor. They should be put in a bowl or basin. There are also hanging cages called suet cages available for vegetables which allow the birds to peck at the treat. Some vegetables can be hung as they are, while others are better placed in the bowl, bucket or suet cage.

Apples - can contain cyanide but not enough to cause fatality.

Asparagus - can be fed but the chickens may not like it.

Bananas - unpeeled bananas are high in potassium.

Beans - if well cooked can be given as a treat

Bread - most kinds can be fed as an occasional treat
Broccoli - can be fed as a treat

Chapter 5: Feeding

Brussels Sprouts - whole head can be fed

Cauliflower - occasional treat

Cabbage - whole head can be fed

Carrots - can be given raw or cooked

Cat food - both dry and tinned cat food can be fed in moderation during molting. Should not be fed to chicks. Over feeding cat food can be harmful.

Cereal - whole grain cereals, not sugared cereal

Cheese - Feed occasionally. Provides protein and calcium. Cottage cheese can also be fed

Corn - tinned or on the cob can be fed, raw or cooked

Crickets - live crickets can be fed. Provide protein

Cucumbers - flesh and seeds can be fed

Fish/ seafood - must be cooked

Flowers - untreated by pesticides, not florist's flowers

Fruit - such as pears, peaches, cherries without the stones

Grains - such as flax etc. can be fed

Grapes - seedless only. Can be cut in half for younger birds

Leftovers - only if still fit for human consumption

Lettuce - can be a big treat

Kale - other leafy greens can also be given as a treat

Chapter 5: Feeding

Meal worms - can be bought in pet stores. Most chickens like these

Melon - seeds and flesh can be given

Oatmeal/porridge - raw or cooked, though cooked has higher nutritional value.

Pasta - Little nutritional value but can be given

Peas - can be given

Peppers - bell peppers can be given as an occasional treat.

Pomegranates - can be given raw

Popcorn - must be popped without salt, syrup or butter

Potatoes - must be cooked without green peel. Sweet potatoes must also be cooked.

Pumpkins - seeds and flesh can be given raw or cooked. Does contain nutritional value

Raisins - can be give occasionally

Rice - Must be cooked. White rice has very little nutritional value

Scratch - this is cracked corn with grains such as wheat, oats or rye mixed in. This is not a complete feed. Given as a treat to encourage scratching behaviors and provide entertainment.

Sprouts - wheat and oat sprouts can be given

Sunflower seeds - shelled or un-shelled can be given

Tomatoes - raw or cooked tomatoes can be given

Chapter 5: Feeding

Turnips - can be given cooked

Watermelon - seeds and flesh can be given

Yogurt - both plain and flavored yogurt can be fed but plain is better. This can be good for the digestive system.

Chapter 6: Home Made Feed

1) How to Make Your Own Feed

Many beginner chicken owners prefer to buy commercial complete chicken feed, though some chicken owners advocate mixing a home made chicken feed. The benefits are that you have complete control over what the chickens eat and you will know exactly what foodstuffs are going into their systems. It may be money saving, but this would be a small amount and probably shouldn't be taken into consideration. The disadvantages are that the mixing of food needs to be exact. You have to consider whether the ingredients are available at all times or whether some are seasonal. The nutritional composition needs to be considered: the feed will need to meet the nutritional requirements of the chickens. Will you be able to make up a big enough quantity? Will you be able to use a local mill to mix the feed or will the purchase of a mixer be necessary to do it on site? If you are capable of mixing large quantities of feed, how and where will it be stored?

2) Starter Feed

Here is a general table for composition of home made feed, however, each ingredient may provide a differing nutritional value depending on the time of year or ground it was grown on. This means that the information given here will not be exact and some chemical analysis may be necessary to sure correct amounts of protein and other nutrients. This table would make 45 kg or 100 lb of feed.

Chapter 6: Home Made Feed

INGREDIENT	KILOGRAMS	POUNDS
Coarsely ground grain such as corn, barley oats, wheat, milo	20.5	46
Wheat bran, mill feed, rice bran	4.5	10
Soya bean meal, cottonseed meal, sesame meal, peanut meal	13	29
Meat meal, fish meal, soya bean meal	2.3	5
Alfalfa meal (unnecessary for free range)	1.8	4
Bone meal, defluorinated dicalcium phosphate	1	2
Vitamin supplement - vitamin A, vitamin D3, riboflavin, or yeast, milk powder	1	2
Ground limestone, marble, oyster shell	0.5	1
Trace mineral salt or iodized salt supplemented with 15mg (0.5 oz) manganese sulphate and 15mg (0.5) zinc oxide	200g	0.5
Total	45	100

Chapter 6: Home Made Feed

3) Grower Feed

Here is a general table for composition of home made feed, however, each ingredient may provide a differing nutritional value depending on the time of year or ground it was grown on. This means that the information given here will not be exact and some chemical analysis may be necessary to sure correct amounts of protein and other nutrients. This table would make 45 kg or 100 lb of feed.

INGREDIENT	KILOGRAMS	POUNDS
Coarsely ground grain such as corn, barley oats, wheat, milo	22.5	50
Wheat bran, mill feed, rice bran	8	18
Soya bean meal, cottonseed meal, sesame meal, peanut meal	7	16
Meat meal, fish meal, soya bean meal	2.3	5
Alfalfa meal (unnecessary for free range)	1.8	4
Bone meal, defluorinated dicalcium phosphate	1	2
Vitamin supplement - vitamin A, vitamin D3, riboflavin, or yeast, milk powder	1	2
Ground limestone, marble, oyster shell	1	2

Chapter 6: Home Made Feed

Trace mineral salt or iodized salt supplemented with 15mg (0.5 oz) manganese sulphate and 15mg (0.5) zinc oxide	200g	0.5
Total	45	100

4) Layer Feed

Here is a general table for composition of home made feed, however, each ingredient may provide a differing nutritional value depending on the time of year or ground it was grown on. This means that the information given here will not be exact and some chemical analysis may be necessary to sure correct amounts of protein and other nutrients. This table would make 45 kg or 100 lb of feed.

INGREDIENT	KILOGRAMS	POUNDS
Coarsely ground grain such as corn, barley oats, wheat, milo	24	53.5
Wheat bran, mill feed, rice bran	7.5	17
Soya bean meal, cottonseed meal, sesame meal, peanut meal	6.7	15
Meat meal, fish meal, soya bean meal	1.3	3
Alfalfa meal (unnecessary for free range)	1.8	4

Chapter 6: Home Made Feed

Bone meal, defluorinated dicalcium phosphate	1	2
Vitamin supplement - vitamin A, vitamin D3, riboflavin, or yeast, milk powder	1	2
Ground limestone, marble, oyster shell	1.3	3
Trace mineral salt or iodized salt supplemented with 15mg (0.5 oz) manganese sulphate and 15mg (0.5) zinc oxide	200g	0.5
Total	45	100

There are books available with more details on homemade feed but, as stated before, it does need to be exact and is problematic and time consuming. Most chicken owners and experts strongly advise against it, and advocate commercial feed. Also the chemical analysis of the nutritional content may not be feasible as it can be expensive. Commercial feeds are complete and balanced.

Chapter 7: Health

1) Vaccinations

The local veterinarian will be able to advise you on vaccinations depending on which diseases are prevalent in your area. The hatchery will have vaccinated any chickens they sell with a standard round of vaccinations. This may mean that your flock has received vaccination that it will not need or the flock may not have received vaccinations that they will need. Always ask your vet for help and advice. There are a range of vaccines available but the most common vaccines are for Marek's disease, salmonella, Infectious Bronchitis (IB), Avian RhinoTracheitis (ART) and Mycoplasma gallisepticum (MG). Vaccines introduce the virus into the system, the bird will then begin to build an immunity to the virus. Vaccines will not cause the illness itself but they imitate the illness. The choice to vaccinate is up to the individual and depends on the area, the holding itself and the flock. Some chicken owners do not vaccinate backyard chickens as hygiene and proper care can help immensely to prevent disease. However, other diseases can be carried by insects etc, and if there is disease in your area, it is advisable to vaccinate.

2) Signs of Ill Health

There are some signs to watch for which can indicate that a chicken is in bad health. Firstly, a pale comb can be a sign of ill health. The bird can be drowsy and weak, unusually tame, reluctant or unable to walk and move around. If a bird which normally roosts, stays on the ground at night, then this may be a sign of illness. The bird may have its feathers fluffed up and its head down or tucked under a wing. The eyes may be cloudy or swollen, have cloudy spots on the pupils or there may be a discharge from the eyes. There may be a nasal discharge or scabby, crusted nostrils. The bird may be panting with the beak open, fluid can be running from the mouth or the breathing may be labored. There may be sores, red or blackened areas on the skin. There may be diarrhea and it can be green, white or bloody. The feathers in the vent area may be clumped, and the vent area can be sore, swollen or distended. The bird may have stopped or reduced its eating and drinking. It may be a lot less active than it normally would be. Hens may stop producing their normal rate of eggs or the eggs may be poorly shaped or colored. If your bird begins to exhibit any behaviors that are not normal for her, then it can indicate that there is something wrong.

3) Common Poisons

There are several substances which chickens will view as food. The human caretaker may not realize that there are common dangers to the birds which are easily overlooked and readily available in most backyards.
If the birds find some widely scattered granular fertilizer they may eat one or two bits and then move on. However, if they see the fertilizer being scattered, they may compete with each other and eat quite a lot before being chased away or leaving of their own accord. They may become excited if they find a large amount of fertilizer in a bucket and eat more than they should. Granular fertilizer can look quite similar to their feed. Fertilizers should be kept locked up in a place where the birds and any children cannot get to them. The chickens should be locked up before any fertilizer is spread.
If you use pesticides to kill weeds then the chickens should be kept away from any areas where it has been used. Pesticides can be fatal if the birds even get some on their feet. Commonly used garden poisons such as snail and slug bait are most often in pellet form and are extremely toxic.
Mice and rat poison are fatal to chickens if ingested. Deceased mice and rats that have been poisoned should not be ingested either. Poisons should be placed in places where neither chickens nor

Chapter 7: Health

children can get access to them.
If you are using plant seeds which have been treated with fungicides or other pesticides, it is important to make sure that the chickens cannot get access to them when they are stored or after planting. It is possible that the birds will scratch up and eat seeds so it may be a good idea to fence off any area where these types of seeds have been planted.

Paint flakes from old buildings can be extremely dangerous. Older paint can be lead-based which can cause lead poisoning. Lead poisoning is quite slow and it can be hard to realize the connection between the illness and the ingestion of paint flakes. Also it is important not to leave any open cans of paint near the chickens. Generally chickens who have free range access are very good at knowing which berries and vegetation should not be eaten. Caged chickens or chickens without outdoor access are much more likely to eat something poisonous. This is because they usually don't have as much variety or fresh food.

4) Injuries

There are many ways in which a chicken can become injured. However every injury, minor or major, is a risk, as chickens can die from stress and shock when injured, rather than as a result of the injury. If a chicken has been injured, it must be carefully inspected as feathers can hide injuries, particularly injuries which may not bleed much. The stress and shock must be reduced as much as possible. Do not chase the injured bird. It is possible that the bird will hide in the coop as they sometimes head for home when stressed. Close the bird in the coop and allow it to settle. Then catch the bird with as little fuss and as calmly as possible. The bird should be kept in a dark, safe place to help calm it. If it is cold, there should be a heat source but the bird should have enough room to move away if it gets too hot.

The bird should be checked often to ensure that it isn't too hot, especially a bird who can not move well. Offer water immediately, although food should not be given for a few hours after the injury.

Chapter 7: Health

If the injury is bleeding, the bird should be removed and isolated from the flock, as the flock can pick on an injured and bleeding bird. Also, the handler should be gentle, careful and should wear gloves in case of disease. When examining the bird for injury, the feathers should be parted, blood should be cleaned, and loose clumped feathers should be removed.

Skin injuries, wounds, cuts and punctures
The skin of a chicken is thin and can tear easily. If it is a shallow wound, the area should be washed and patted dry, or cleaned with hydrogen peroxide. If it continues to bleed, apply a blood stopping or styptic powder or pressure to stop the flow. Styptic powder is not expensive and it is advisable to keep some on hand. It can be bought at pet stores, agricultural stores or online. Bandages generally do not stay on chickens - partly because of the feathers and partly because the bird will pull them off. If the cut is on the foot, the bird should be kept on a very clean surface for a few days.

Animal bites
Animals bites can be incredibly dangerous for a chicken. It is probable that the wound, regardless of severity, will become infected. In most cases of a puncture through the head or body cavity, it is nearly always kinder to euthanize the bird. In some cases, the best course of action is to contact the vet immediately. If the wound is minor, it should be washed with warm water and then flushed with hydrogen peroxide, betadine or iodine. The chicken should be kept in a clean, quiet area. The wound must be checked several times per day for signs of infection, and cleaned two to three times per day. It may be possible to put a wound dressing on if the weather is warm and the area cannot be reached by the beak. The dressing will prevent flies from laying eggs on the wound. Wound dressings can be found in pet stores, agricultural stores or the veterinarian will also have them.

Foot sores
Foot sores are also known as bumblefoot. Bumblefoot is a bacterial infection of the foot. It is most often seen in heavy

Chapter 7: Health

rooster but is not unheard of in other chickens. It is caused by a cut or scratch which becomes contaminated. It causes a swelling and can feel soft at the early stages and then become hard to the touch. It can look inflamed, red and can feel hot. A black scab can form over the sore. It can be painful and make the bird limp or not walk at all. If it goes untreated it can cause death. The bacteria which causes bumblefoot can infect humans so always wear gloves when examining a chicken with it or suspected to have it.

Any infected birds must be isolated from the flock and kept in a clean place with a soft litter, such as pine shavings. Antibiotics may clear up the infection. A vet or some agricultural stores will sell them. Make sure the instructions on the antibiotic are followed carefully and the full course is given. Soaking the foot can also help. This should be done as well as the antibiotic treatment. A cup of Epsom Salt with warm water makes a good soak. The water should be warm but should not burn a hand or a chicken foot. Hold the foot in the water for ten to fifteen minutes. Soaking will soften the abscess so that the scab can gently be removed. The wound should be opened by gently pulling the edges apart, then rinsed with hydrogen peroxide. Any pus should be cleaned out. A bird safe antibiotic ointment should be applied with a gauze pad covering it. The gauze can be secured using tape or vet-wrap, which is a bandage which sticks to itself.

This should be done once a day until it begins to heal. All discarded dressings and the water for soaking the foot should be discarded very carefully. If the edges of the wound will not pull apart, call the vet. Some birds can have diarrhea when on antibiotics so it is a good idea to add some yogurt to the diet.

Torn and/or infected comb or wattle.
Combs and wattles can become torn or damaged. They cannot usually be repaired and can become infected. They should be trimmed. This can either be done at the vet or at home. If you are doing it at home, first wash the area and clean it with rubbing alcohol. Trim the torn area with sterilized scissors or a sterilized knife. Apply an antibiotic cream to the edges. If the weather is

Chapter 7: Health

warm apply an antibiotic fly ointment to prevent flies from laying eggs in the wound.

The bird should be isolated from the flock until the wound has healed. There may be some bleeding when trimming but it should be minor. This process will be painful but it will be over quickly.

Eye injuries

If a bird has an eye injury, it should be cleaned with an un-medicated eyewash and the bird isolated from the flock. A chicken with one blind eye is usually fine but if the blindness is in both eyes, the bird will need to be permanently separated from the flock and kept enclosed.

Beak injuries

Beaks can be broken or damaged. Chickens can live naturally without small portions of the beak but large portions are much more difficult to survive without. It may become impossible for the bird to eat. The beak will not grow back and it may be kinder to euthanize the bird, although it is certainly possible for the bird to be hand fed rather than feed itself.

Broken wings and legs

Broken wings are fairly easy to overcome. If a bone has broken through the skin, it is probable that infection will occur. Broken wings and legs can be amputated by the vet but the quality of life for a chicken with one leg is poor. A broken wing may look twisted or it may be dragging on the ground. It can be treated by strapping the wing in a natural position with vet-wrap and gauze for around two weeks. The bird should be separated from the flock for this time and the wing may heal crooked or drooped. A broken leg can look swollen and crooked. A vet can splint it and a young bird will heal fairly quickly. The bird should be kept separate from the flock until it has healed.

Frostbite

Frostbite can cause blackened areas on the combs, wattles, ear lobes and toes. Most often, the affected area will dry out and fall off. If infection sets in, the area may need to be trimmed and an antibiotic cream should be applied. If there is no infection, do not trim the blackened areas as they provide some protection to the area beneath. Heat lamps can help, but the temperature should be carefully monitored as over heating can cause moisture in the air which can cause problems of its own. Roosters with frostbite may become temporarily infertile. This is not because of the frostbite but is caused by the temperature. Fertility is normally restored once the temperature warms and the rooster recovers from the stress.

Egg bound
When a hen has an egg which she cannot lay she is said to be egg bound. Proper feeding, handling and care minimizes the risk of egg binding. In domestic hens, egg binding usually only occurs due to a genetic defect or when hens are injured. Old hens, or hens that are weakened by poor feed, worms, disease or severe cold can become egg bound. Egg binding is very dangerous for the hen. The hen will sit on the floor or ground. The feathers will be fluffed up and the hen will be drowsy. You may see the hen strain to lay the egg. The safest way to help the hen is to put her in a wire cage with a bowl of warm, steaming water underneath. The steam should be warm but not burning. A heat lamp should be above the cage and the cage should be wrapped with a blanket or plastic. This will keep the heat in but care must be taken to make sure it does not get too hot. There should be free access to water. It may take a few hours for the hen to pass the egg. If she has laid the egg, she will have perked up considerably. If there is no egg and she is more alert and active, then it is unlikely she is egg bound. If the hen has not changed, keep her in the cage for a few more hours. An egg bound hen will die within 48 hours if the egg does not pass. A vet may be able to give the hen an injection to help the hen pass the egg.   Once a hen has become egg bound, it is likely it will happen again. Rough handling just before an egg is to be laid can cause the egg to break in the hen. This can cause infection and death. Always handle hens carefully just before laying time.

Chapter 7: Health

5) Parasites

Parasites are common in all breeds and in all locations. Free range chickens can be less likely to have lice but they can be more likely to have internal parasites. If the chickens are frequently handled then it is a good idea to treat them for parasites.

Worms
Worms are a common internal parasite and they can become dangerous if the chicken is already ill or lives in a low hygiene environment. It is believed that chickens with a worm infestation are more likely to be cannibalistic, retain eggs, have poor egg production, poor size and color of egg, poor growth and in extreme cases, die. The chicken may have an increased appetite and weight loss. To diagnose worms a sample of the dropping should be sent to the vet for analysis. There are several different types of worm.

Roundworm
Roundworm eggs can be ingested when foraging. The eggs hatch in the intestine and are passed out through the droppings. The worms are up to three inches long and white. Occasionally, a worm can enter the oviduct. It can be wrapped in the eggshell and laid with the egg. Over the counter bird wormers available from the vet can control roundworm. The shell of a roundworm egg is extremely tough. Many disinfectants won't kill roundworm so ask your vet to recommend a brand which will help. They can remain in the environment for a very long period of time so good hygiene practice is important. A routine worming schedule can also be set up which will prevent any infestation at all.

Tapeworm
Tapeworm can be ingested along with earthworms, snails, slugs, grasshoppers and some varieties of flies and beetles. These food items to chickens are intermediate hosts to the tapeworm. The larvae mature and produce eggs in the intestines of the chicken which are passed out through the droppings. They can occasionally be seen in the droppings but as this does not happen

often and there are generally no other symptoms, most people are unaware that the chickens have tapeworms. Tapeworms can be treated with a wormer, though there is not a specific one for chickens. Always consult a veterinarian to get the correct dose.

Gapeworm
Gapeworms also need an intermediate host. They are more likely to be found in chickens that are free range or in pasture pens. They are more dangerous than other worms as they attach to the trachea. This can cause difficult breathing. The chicken may try to breathe with its mouth open and may make a grunting sound. Like tapeworm treatment, there is no specific gapeworm treatment for chickens and you should contact a vet for the proper dosing instructions.

Coccidiosis
Chickens can be infected by nine different types of Coccidia, the internal parasite which cause coccidiosis. The immature coccidia are known as oocysts. These can be spread by shoes, clothing, wild animals, pests, vermin and infected chickens. The coccidia line the intestines and they can damage the intestinal wall causing bleeding and interfere with nutrient absorption from food. They most often affect younger birds, though occasionally, they can be a problem in older birds. Chicks under three weeks rarely show symptoms. From three to thirty weeks, the symptoms include anemia, dehydration, reduced appetite, pale skin, drowsiness, inactivity, and bloody diarrhea. There are treatments available and there is medicated chick feed.

Lice
Lice are an external parasite. There are several types of lice which can feed on chickens. Chicken lice do not feed on the blood, but on the feather or shed skin cells. They are long, narrow insects that can move quickly. The lice eggs are tiny dots on the feathers. The chicken needs to be treated with a medicated dust bath which must be obtained from a vet.

Mites

Mites do feed on the blood, although a few types eat feathers. The blood feeding mites will burrow into the skin. The can cause anemia, reduced egg production and damage to the skin and feather. The Northern Fowl mite will stay on the bird for the lifetime. It can cause scabs, anemia and is uncomfortable for the bird. The Common Chicken mite feeds at night and will hide in the cracks of surfaces throughout the day. The Scaly Leg mite is found in between the skin scales of the legs. They cause the leg to look thick and scabbed as they cause the skin scale to protrude. They can be treated by covering the leg with petroleum jelly, mineral oil or linseed oil as this will smother the mite. Both the birds and the environment need to be treated for mites.

Fowl tick

Ticks feed on the blood of the chicken. In colder areas, it is unusual to see larger numbers of tick as the cold kills them. They are more prevalent in warmer areas. They feed at night and once finished they drop off the bird and hide. They cause anemia, weakness, weight loss and reduced egg production. To treat ticks, the environment is treated rather than the bird. The housing should be sprayed, and any weeds and debris should be removed. Any pasture should be treated. A vet can recommend and advise on which products to use.

Chiggers

Chiggers are from a family of mite and are sometimes called harvest mites. They attach to the breast, wings or legs of the chicken and will eat until full. The bite site can be intensely itchy and leaves red spots as the mite injects a substance as it feeds. The chicken can become ill, lose appetite, not want to drink, keep the feathers fluffed and scratch a lot. As with other mites, it is important to treat the environment. Chickens can pick up chiggers from grassy areas, hay or straw.

6) Common Diseases

There are a few general signs of illness and disease to look out for.

Chapter 7: Health

If you have any doubts as to the health of your chickens it is advisable to contact your vet.

Avian Pox
This is also called fowl pox. It is a viral disease that can be contracted through the bite of a blood sucking insect, chickens who have the disease and contaminated surfaces. There is a vaccine available. Birds who have recovered do not carry the disease. The symptoms include white spots on the skin, scabby sores on the comb, white membranes and ulcers in the mouth and trachea, and cessation of egg production. Fowl pox can affect chickens of any age. The affected bird should be kept warm and dry and fed soft food. Many birds can recover if given the appropriate treatment and level of care.

Botulism
Botulism is a bacterial by product and is contracted by eating food or drinking water which has been infected with it. There is no available vaccine. The source of the infection needs to be found and removed. This may be a decaying carcass, or some meat left near water, or insects who have fed on the meat or the water. The symptoms include tremors which quickly turn to paralysis. Eventually the respiration system becomes paralyzed. The feathers are easily pulled and death can occur within a few hours. There is an antitoxin available from a veterinarian but it can be very expensive. If the disease is found early, a teaspoon of Epsom salts dissolved in one ounce of warm water then dripped into the crop several times per day may help.

Fowl Cholera
Fowl cholera is a bacterial disease which is transmitted through wild animals and birds. It can also be transmitted bird to bird, and on contaminated soil, shoes, equipment, clothing, water and food. There is a vaccine but it has to be administered by a specially trained representative of the Department of Agriculture. It usually affects bird over four months old. The symptoms include a green-yellow diarrhea, respiration difficulties, swollen joints, darkened coloring of head and wattles and it can be fatal. It does

not affect humans. There is no treatment. As recovered birds will be a carrier and could infect others, all infected birds must be destroyed.

Infectious Bronchitis
Infectious bronchitis is a very contagious viral disease which is spread through the air, contact and contaminated surfaces. There is a vaccine but it must be given to hens under fifteen weeks old as it will cause egg production to stop. The symptoms include coughing, sneezing, cessation of egg production and a watery discharge from the nose. There is a fifty per cent mortality rate in chicks under six weeks.

Infectious Coryza
Infectious coryza is a bacterial disease which can be contracted though carrier birds, infected water and contaminated surfaces. There is no vaccine available. The symptoms include a swollen head, comb and wattle, cessation of egg production, a sticky discharge from the eyes and nose, moist area under the wings and the eyes can be swollen shut. There is no treatment. Infected birds must be destroyed as they will remain carriers.

Marek's Disease
Marek's disease is a highly contagious viral disease. It is contracted by inhalation of skin cells or feather dust of carrier birds. There is a vaccine available which is administered to day old chicks. The symptoms include internal and external tumors, paralysis, change of iris color to gray and the eyes not reacting to light. It usually affects birds under twenty weeks old. There is no treatment. Marek's disease has a high death rate and any survivors would be carriers who would infect healthy birds.

Moniliasis
Moniliasis is also known as thrush. It is a fungal disease which is contracted through moldy food, water and contaminated surfaces. It can also occur after antibiotic treatment. There is no vaccine . The symptoms include poor laying, white crusty vent area, ruffled feathers, inflammation in vent area, increased appetite, and white

Chapter 7: Health

cheesy substance in the crop. It is treated with an anti-fungal medication which can be obtained from the vet. The feed and water should be removed and replaced and the containers must be disinfected.

Mycoplasmosis
Mycoplasmosis is also known as CRD and Air Sac Disease. It is contracted through wild birds and can be transmitted from an infected hen through the egg to a chick. There is a vaccine available. The symptoms include weakness and poor laying in a mild case, and respiration problems, coughing, sneezing, swollen and infected joints and death in its more acute forms. It can be treated with antibiotics. A vet should be contacted immediately.

Newcastle Disease
Newcastle disease is a very contagious viral disease. It is contracted through infected birds - both domestic and wild, and it can be carried on shoes, clothing and surfaces. There is a vaccine. The symptoms include wheezing, respiration difficulties, nasal discharge, cessation of laying, cloudy eyes, paralysis in the legs and wings and twisted heads and necks. There is no treatment. Young birds will usually die but older birds may recover. Recovered birds are not carriers.

Omphalitis
Omphalitis is also known as Mushy Chick. It can be found in newly hatched chicks. It is a bacterial infection of the navel from unclean surfaces or a weak immune system. It can spread from chick to chick on contaminated surfaces. There is no available vaccine. The symptoms include an inflamed navel area, a bad odor, drowsiness, weakness, an enlarged abdomen and bluish abdominal muscles. Antibiotics and clean, disinfected housing may help sometimes but most chicks with this disease will die. It is important to remove all healthy chicks to other clean housing immediately and to use caution when handling affected chicks as the bacteria which causes this can infect humans.

Chapter 7: Health

Pullorum
Pullorum is a viral disease which is contracted through carrier birds and contaminated surfaces, shoes and clothing. There is no available vaccine. There is a blood test to identify carriers. The symptoms in chicks include inactivity, white diarrhea, crusted vent area, and respiration difficulties. Some chicks may die without displaying any symptoms. The symptoms in older birds include coughing, sneezing and poor laying. Most chicks that have been infected will die. Recovered birds will be carriers and will infect other birds. All infected birds must be destroyed.

7) Prevention of Disease

It is important to prevent disease rather than cure it. Good hygiene practices can help. Having a preventative worming program can also help. Some chicken owners like to worm twice a year, whether or not the chickens are displaying signs of worms. Replacing the food and water every few days ensures that it does not become moldy or stale. Any new birds should be purchased from a reputable hatchery and they should be vaccinated before purchase. If you hatch your own chicks, you will have to decide whether or not to vaccinate. It is worth knowing the vital signs of your chicken. Temperature generally falls between 105 -109 degrees Fahrenheit or 40 to 42 degrees Celsius.

The heart rate is normally around 280 - 315 beat per minute and the respiration rate is around 18 - 20 breaths per minute for a rooster and 30 - 35 breaths per minute for a hen. Each chicken may have slightly varying vital signs. Some chicken owners keep a record of the different vital signs of each bird which can help to show if there is a difference. Of course this is not possible on a large scale operation so the general number can provide a good guide.

8) Hygiene

As said before, good hygiene can help prevent disease and illness. Hygiene involves cleaning the coop, the feeders, drinkers and any

Chapter 7: Health

areas the chickens have access to. It is not a good idea to wet anything which will not dry by nightfall. If you are going to disinfect any areas, then rinse them with clean water afterwards. You will need a shovel, rake, a broom, a muck bucket and a dust mask. You can also use a vacuum cleaner, work gloves, a hose and a dustpan. It is not necessary to use cleaning products but some chicken owners prefer to use one to clean the housing and equipment as part of the cleaning routine. If you choose to use a cleaning product, then some household ones can be fine to use but anything with ammonia is not. Read all labels to ensure that the cleaners are safe for pets. After cleaning disinfect the area and equipment.

Some chicken owners prefer to keep all areas immaculate. If you live in an urban or suburban area then this is probably a good idea. Other owners are more laid back and will do the bulk of the cleaning once a month. In rural areas however, it is possible to use deep litter. Deep litter means that the litter is removed once or twice per year, with minimal maintenance between. The litter must be dry and loose. Fresh litter should be put down on top of the old and the area must be well ventilated. The litter may need to be moved around with a rake to make sure it doesn't get compacted, hard or crusty. The wet litter may need to be removed and replaced. Some studies have shown that chickens raised in deep litter are more parasite and disease resistant. This method is unsuitable for chickens in urban settings.

Other chicken owners place a board under the roost. The area under the roost is usually where the highest accumulation of droppings lie. The board can be removed and cleaned regularly but the whole house does not need cleaned as frequently.
At the very least, chickens need dry space, clean litter, clean food, clean water and clean nest boxes. To keep the water and food containers clean they will need to be cleaned more often than any other equipment. Brush out any leftover or caked feed. Wash and rinse them. You may want to soak them in a solution of one part bleach to three parts water, or use a disinfectant. They should then be rinsed. Leave containers to dry in the sun but make sure they

Chapter 7: Health

are completely dry before refilling. Any water containers or automatic drinkers should be checked for algae, slime and rust. Depending on the area, there may also be hard water build up. A toothbrush can be a great tool for cleaning the smaller areas of automatic drinkers.

Nest boxes should be kept as clean as possible. Bedding should be replaced frequently. However, a hen who is sitting on eggs in a nest box should be left alone if possible. The area around the nest can have dirty material removed and droppings can be removed but the whole box cannot be cleaned until the eggs have hatched. It is a good idea to do a deep clean once or twice a year, whether in a urban or rural setting. Make sure the chickens are not in the house and begin by scraping off the roosts. Dust or vacuum the cobwebs. Brush down the walls and take out all the litter. There may be dust and some chicken owners find that damping the litter with water helps reduce the amount of dust. The floor should be swept with a damp broom and light bulbs should be wiped to clear off dust. If there are windows, they will need to be cleaned. Any fans need the blades and the outer housing cleaned. Then put fresh litter in the house.

It is also necessary to clean and weed any outdoor areas that the chickens have access to. Any droppings can be removed to a compost heap. However, in some areas this may not be possible. Depending on the regulations in your area, you may have to bury it, leave with lawn waste for collection or take it to a landfill.

9) Keeping a Healthy Flock

There are a few things that can cause a chicken to become sick. It is the job and responsibility of the chicken owner to make sure that these do not happen. This means taking some basic precautions and trying to keep stress levels low as much as possible. For example your birds will need protecting from extreme heat or extreme cold, the housing needs to be kept dry and any handling or catching must be as stress free as possible.

Chapter 7: Health

Heat
Caged birds do not do well in high temperatures. They can become heat stressed which can be fatal. Free range birds are better at surviving heat because they will find the cool places to hide. Signs of heat stress includes inactivity and breathing through an open mouth. It is important to work slowly and calmly with any birds suffering from heat stress. They should be given unrestricted access to water, and ventilation. The birds won't drink warm water so make sure the water is changed frequently and cool. It may be a good idea to immerse a bird with heat stress in cool but not cold water for a few minutes.

Cold
As long as the shelter is dry and sheltered from wind, chickens are better able to cope with cold in comparison to heat. However they can be affected by frostbite in the comb, wattles and even the toes. Frostbite causes blackened areas which may eventually fall off. Breeds with small combs and wattles cope much better in cold climates because smaller appendages do not lose as much body heat and do not get frostbitten as easily. It can also be a good idea to have wide roosts because this allows the birds to sit with flat feet which means the feathers can cover the toes.

The birds will also need more feed in cold weather to help continued body function. The birds may stop laying in cold weather or, if they continue to lay, the weather may contribute to egg binding. It is very important that the birds have access to water. If there is a danger of ice then the water should be refilled twice daily or a heated water dish can be used.

Damp
Damp and wet conditions can be a big factor in the illness of chickens. Damp can be caused by moisture which comes from the bird's respiration and fecal matter, in housing with poor ventilation or from the rain or snow. Warm air can hold a lot of moisture. If a coop is overheated in cold weather, condensation will form which can cause wet and unhealthy conditions. Mold and fungus will grow in wet areas. There are a number of illnesses which are

Chapter 7: Health

caused by mold on the feed and bedding. The bedding should always be dry, the feed should never be moldy and the house should be well ventilated. There should also be adequate drainage for the outdoor run.

Chapter 8: Housing

1) Coops

Chicken housing does not need to be expensive, but the chickens need to be protected from predators, sheltered from the weather, feel secure to lay eggs and roost. There are many types of coop available. The size of the coop will depend on how much space you have available and how many chickens there are in the flock. Each bird will need a minimum of 2 square feet, but 3 or 4 square feet is better. They will also need a minimum of 3 to 6 square foot of outdoor space in the form of a chicken run. They need roost space of around one foot length. The roosts should be a minimum of two foot from the ground and a maximum of five, depending on the breed. They should not be directly above other roosts or the food and water containers. The coop will need nest boxes which should feel dark and secluded.

They should be the same color and size to prevent several hens choosing the same box. If necessary two hens can share a box but if there are more than four to a box they will fight and may begin to lay eggs outside of the box. The minimum size for a nest box is 12 square inches, but 12 x 18 inches or 16 x 16 inches are better sizes. Nest boxes should be in a sheltered and dimly lit area of the house. The hatchery will probably have houses and boxes available for purchase.

The coop must have good ventilation. This can be through windows, roof vents or fans You may want an electrical supply to the coop. This means that there can be lighting, a heat source such as a heater or heat lamps or a cooling fan. If you have electric it is important to check over the fittings as part of the daily routine.

Chapter 8: Housing

Cages
Some chicken owners prefer to house the birds in cages. This method of housing is not suitable for more than ten birds. It is unsuitable for meat birds. It is suitable for laying and show breeds. It can create more work for the care provider and it can also stop normal behaviors but can cause abnormal behaviors. Cages are most often made from wire mesh but there are two flooring options. The floors can also be wire mesh or can be solid wood or metal. The solid floor should be removable for cleaning which can be time consuming. The wire flooring can cause bumblefoot particularly in heavy breed roosters.

All in one units.
An all in one unit is essentially a house with a built in fenced yard. The run is attached to the housing as part of it. There should be a door or access area on the outside of the housing away from the run or enclosure area, to allow for human access. This type of housing can be ideal for urban or suburban chicken keepers, but can be expensive. Depending on the size they can be used for up to ten birds but usually they are used for small two to four bird flocks. They are not suitable for meat breeds. They are suitable for laying and show breeds. They can be used in cold weather depending on the material used for construction.

Cage free indoor
Cage free indoor, means that while the birds spend all their time indoors, they are not confined to cages. A section of a barn or garage can be fenced or blocked off. This type of housing is fine as long as there is plenty of space for each bird. It is most often used for larger flock numbers and is suitable for show, layer breeds and meat breeds. It protects from the weather. However, it can be stressful for some breeds.

Tractor
Tractor housing is a coop with a roof but no floor that is easily moved around the yard. The down sides to this type of housing is that it doesn't provide adequate access for feed and water, it is hard to catch the birds if you need to, it is inadequate for cold

Chapter 8: Housing

weather and a large yard is needed so as to provide plenty of space for moving. These coops come in a variety of sizes and can house more than ten birds if the size if large enough. They can be used for layers, meat, show breeds and pullets. Small tractor coops can be carried or pushed, medium size ones usually have wheels but very large ones may need to be pulled by a vehicle when moving.

A-frame
A-frame housing can be movable like tractor housing or stationary like all in one units. They consist of a housing area and an outdoor area. They are shaped like a triangle or an A. They can be covered with metal, wire, plastic or other materials They are most often used as temporary housing during warm weather but if built with other material can be used in colder weather also. Depending on the size they can house more than ten chickens. They are suitable for meat breeds as long as the sizing requirements are met. They are suitable for laying and show breeds. They may need to be anchored in strong winds. Access can be difficult for the human care provider.

Hoop
Hoop housing is similar to A frame, except for the shape. It is shaped like an arch or tunnel which can be covered with wire, metal, plastic or other materials like A-frame housing. It has the same drawbacks and benefits as A-frame housing. Similarly, it may need to be anchored in strong winds. Size is important if considering this housing for meat breeds, but it is suitable for laying and show breeds.

Shelter with outside run
This type of housing is often the most used. The shelter can be large enough to provide human access and has a smaller door for the chickens. The birds are protected by the outdoor enclosure but have enough space to roam. This housing can be as large as necessary. It can be used in cold weather with the right materials and space. The chickens can choose when to go into the shelter and can be safely closed inside at night. It is not the best option

Chapter 8: Housing

for meat breeds but is a good option for laying breeds as well as show breeds. Many chicken owners who start off with an alternative housing method change to this housing method.

Shelter with free range
This housing type is much preferred by most chicken breeds but has its own problems. The birds are more vulnerable to predators. It is not suitable for urban areas or suburban areas as the birds may cross into neighbor's yards. The birds may hide the eggs and they tend to be a little wild and hard to catch and handle. They may peck and forage through the garden which can damage plants. They may defecate on porches, step and patios. The benefits are that the chickens tend to be happier, they find a lot of their food while foraging, there's less cleaning for the carer and they tend to have less lice and mites. It tends not to be the best option for meat breeds, as some of these breeds do not like to forage for their food. It can be used in cold weather depending on the materials used for the house. Depending on the predators and available area, this can be a good option for laying hens who have an established egg laying pattern. It is not suitable for show birds.

Pastured poultry
This is when the birds are given access to a restricted amount of pasture. The pasture must be changed frequently as chickens can be hard on grassland. There are two ways of doing this. The first is to move the birds with the housing through the pasture. The second is to have a separate house in each area and only move the birds. This is suitable for more than ten birds but is not suitable for show or most meat breeds. The benefits are that the birds may need less feed and can get a lot of their nutritional requirement from the ground. The disadvantages are that it can be time consuming to implement the pasture management rotation system that is necessary for this method to work. The birds may be slower growing also.

2) Runs
If the chickens are not free range chickens then they will need a chicken run. Each bird needs a minimum of 3 to 6 square foot of

Chapter 8: Housing

space in the run, but if more space can be allocated it will be better. Again, runs are available for purchase and can be bought separately or with a coop. It is possible to get one which joins up with the coop. The hatchery you choose to buy your chickens from will probably have runs available for purchase.

3) Building Your Own Coop
It can be more expensive to build a coop than buy one. If you have the skills, then there are benefits to building your own. You can choose the layout which suits the flock and available apace more accurately than pre-built coops. You can recycle materials that you already have or you can repair an old shed or even a vehicle to make the house for your chickens. It is recommended to draw a plan before you start to build, with the measurements written down. If you decide to home build the run, then you should use chicken wire as other wires can cause damage to the birds or provide them with a way to escape. The posts and the wire should put at least a foot into the ground. The fence of the height should be a minimum of 7 foot but 9 is better. This will help keep predators out of the run.

Eglus
Eglu is a product designed specifically for small scale back yard chicken owners. It is made by the Omlet company and comes in many sizes, designs, colors and prices. An Eglu is a ready made and portable chicken coop. It can come with a run or without. It comes with drinkers and feeders. It is easy to clean and has a built in nest box with a separate door for egg collection. Many people choose this type of coop because it can be moved around the yard and because of its durability.

4) Feeders, Waterers and Dust Baths

There are many types of feeders available for purchase. There are the more expensive automatic feeders and the cheaper containers. They can be made from plastic, aluminum or galvanized steel. It is important to consider not only your budget but your location, as plastic feeders can freeze and crack. The feeder should hold about

Chapter 8: Housing

a day's worth of food for the flock and be large enough for all the chickens to eat at the same time. Each adult bird should have around 6 inches of feeding space, chicks need shallow containers and around 4 inches of feeding space. If necessary then use more than one feeder If the feed container has a top it may encourage birds to roost on it, but if it doesn't they may use it as a dust bath. If the chickens are very messy with the food the you can set the containers on a large plastic or metal tray to prevent food wastage. The container should never be under a perch or roost to prevent contamination from droppings.

You can also recycle something into a feeder such as an old cake tin. Regardless of what you decide to use as a feeder, it should be easy to clean and if it is an automatic feeder it must be checked for function daily. Feeders must be cleaned on a regular basis. Waterers also come in many types. There are also automatic waterers available. Again, they should be kept clean and kept away from the roosts. The rim should be narrow so that the chickens will not perch on it. The material needs to be resistant to cracks and chips. Plastic and glass are not suitable. Aluminum can be used or something like a dog bowl. There are also nipple systems available. The chicken has to push the nipple to get water. These must be kept clean and any automatic system must be regularly checked for function. Water should always be clean, fresh and readily available. The waterer does not have accommodate all the chickens at the same time.

Chicken like to dust bathe. It helps them to keep clean and cool and can help control lice and ticks. A large flat litter tray filled with sand is a good low cost option for a dust bath. It should be kept outside during good weather but taken in if it begins to rain.

5) Foxes

Foxes will try to get into the chicken run. If they succeed they will kill every bird there but will only take one for food. Proper fencing can help but there are other ways to protect from foxes. There are electric fences available. The fox will sniff the fence

Chapter 8: Housing

and once it gets a shock it generally will not try to get through it. Dogs can also act as a deterrent but the fox may just learn how to avoid the dog. A flashing light will deter foxes in the short term but it needs to be moved around regularly. Llamas which have grown up with the flock are supposed to chase foxes away but unless there is an abundance of space this will not be possible. Many chicken owners believe that an electric fence is the most effective method. Studies have shown that only one or two shocks from the fence are enough to stop the fox from attempting to jump or dig under it. An un-electrified fence needs to be around 8 meters high and if possible with an outwardly sloping top which should prevent the fox from climbing over the wire. It has been shown that even one meter of electrified netting can discourage foxes from attempting entry to the chicken run or house.

Chapter 9: Care and Husbandry

1) Handling Chickens

Studies have shown that around 90% of diseases are introduced to the birds through the human caregiver. Disease can live on shoes, clothing, equipment, surfaces, unwashed hands and car tires. This means that disease can be carried into your flock after you have visited a poultry show or any other flock. There are also diseases which can affect birds and humans. There are some rules to follow to prevent contamination.

If you have been near other birds, it is necessary to, at the very least, wash your hands before caring for your own flock. It would be better to change shoes and clothing as well.
If there has been an outbreak of disease in your area then you should avoid visiting poultry shows and other flocks. If it is necessary to do so, then you should shower and change clothes and shoes before caring for your own flock.
Hands should always be washed thoroughly after handling and caring for your flock.

You should not have chickens near your face.
If you are handling sick or diseased birds it is important to wear latex gloves. This is especially important if you're handling a deceased bird.

If the birds are free range, any fruit and vegetables should be thoroughly washed as they may have become contaminated by the birds' fecal matter. Any outdoor furniture and railings which have been in contact with the chickens should also be kept clean.
The meat and eggs must always be stored correctly. Any surfaces, dishes and utensils that have come into contact with raw poultry meat need to be cleaned very carefully with hot water and the

appropriate cleaning products.
If there are any sick or diseased birds in the flock then they should be quarantined. It is also important to quarantine new birds or birds which have been taken off the property.
Children need to be supervised when handling chickens, eggs or equipment. An adult should ensure that children wash their hands immediately and very carefully.

2) Catching Chickens

Sometimes it may be necessary to catch your chickens. The best way to do this is to wait until night and lift the bird from the roost. If there is usually a light in the house during the night it should be turned off and a flashlight should be used instead. It is important not to disturb the other chickens when doing this.

If you need to catch a bird and cannot wait until night then you should lure it to a small area with all exits blocked off. It is important to move calmly and slowly and to try to grab the legs. Chickens tend to expect to be grabbed from above, so grabbing the legs surprises them. There are nets and catching sticks available to purchase. However, nets tend to scare chickens and it can take a lot of practice to use a catching stick. A catching stick has a hook which is placed past the feet and then pulled back to snag the feet and bring the bird to the person operating the stick.

While adult birds should be caught by the leg, chicks should never be caught by the leg. If the chick is in a brooder, one hand should be put in front of the chick and the other should be used to sweep the chick into the first hand. The other method is to put a hand over the back of the chick but this can scare them as it resembles the movements of predators.

Chickens will often try to escape. Usually after escaping they will not go far, unless they are very scared or are not used to the area. If a single bird has escaped it will generally remain close to the flock. If the whole flock escapes, the first thing to do is check for and fix the escape route before attempting to get them back inside.

Chapter 9: Care and Husbandry

Chasing the birds is not a good idea and should be the last resort. If there is a special bucket used for feeding or treats, it should be filled and shown to the flock. If they are interested, it can be used to lure the birds back to the pen. The feed or treats should be put inside to encourage the birds to go inside and then the door can be closed. If the birds will not go inside the pen, try to enclose them in any available space. Chickens tend to want to go back to familiar place before nightfall. Usually they will go back into their house to roost easily. However, if the escaped bird hasn't returned home by nightfall, watch it from a distance to see where it roosts and then you can catch it in the dark.

If the chicken has escaped somewhere that is not familiar to it, if possible let it settle and relax. In these instances it is often quicker and easier to use the net or a catching stick. It is important, however, to make sure that the bird's attention is on something else like feed or other birds. Chickens tend to get easier to catch as they age particularly if they have bonded well with the caretaker. Some breeds are easier to catch due to their friendlier and calmer dispositions. If all other methods of catching the bird fails, then traps such as a box and string or a live trap may be the best method to use.

3) Carrying Chickens

It is only birds that are being taken to slaughter that are carried by the legs with the head hanging down. This is because carrying with this method can hurt the birds or dislocate the legs. The bird should be tucked under one arm with the free hand holding both feet or it can be cradled in the arms, with the wings under an arm. The head can either be forward or backward facing depending on which works best for the caretaker. Most birds can be calmed by talking or gently squeezing.

If the bird is being restrained for treatment by a single person, it can be a good idea to tie the birds legs together, restrain the wings with one hand and lay it on the table or it can be loosely wrapped in a towel to restrain the wings. Some chicken owners prefer to hold

Chapter 9: Care and Husbandry

the birds with their knees while kneeling, with the bird's feet pointed upwards and the head of the bird facing away from the caretaker.

It is important that birds are not squeezed too hard while carrying or restraining as they need movement in their ribs to be able to breathe properly. This means that even if the mouth and nose are uncovered, a bird that is held too tightly can still suffocate. This often happens when children are holding baby chicks. A chick should be held loosely in a closed hand with the head peeking through the fingers.

If a bird is becoming highly stressed by the process of being carried or held, then you should cover its head loosely with a towel, soft cloth or a hood. Doing this should settle and relax the bird. You should always carry one bird at a time. Extra care should be taken when handling roosters because the spurs can cause damage to the arms. It is a good idea to wear long sleeves when handling roosters. You should always remember to wear gloves when handling sick or diseased chickens.

4) Stress and Chickens

One of the effects of stress is that it can lower the immune system and it can cause undesirable and bad behavior. It is important to always try to keep the environment of the chickens as stress free as possible and to reduce the stress when necessary.

Molting
This is when the feathers fall out and are replaced. It usually happens as the days get shorter in the fall but it can be triggered by lack of food. The first molt usually happens after a year of laying. It usually takes 4 to 8 weeks and most birds will not lay eggs during this time. Some breeds have a quick molt which is barely noticeable. These breeds are most often high producing egg laying breeds. There are also individual differences in the length of the molt. Quick molting hens are usually the healthiest and most productive birds in the flock.

The molt begins with the primary feathers of the wings and the feathers on the head. It then moves backwards gradually. However,

Chapter 9: Care and Husbandry

birds shouldn't look bald during this process. The last feathers are replaced with pin feathers which eventually open into new feathers.

It takes a lot of energy for molting and feather growing, so extra feed should be given during this time. The diet for this time should includes good quality protein. Some chicken owners will switch their birds to a meat bird feed during the molt as it contains a higher protein ratio. If you use a good quality complete feed, it should be unnecessary to supplement this with anything else. However, if you use a homemade feed, you may need to increase the protein ratio for molting.

The birds should behave normally during molting. Most birds stop laying eggs although some may lay a few. This is because the energy needs to be focused on growing feathers and not laying eggs. The first eggs after molting may be smaller than usual but they will go back to normal size quite quickly. If a bird seems to be sick or isn't eating or drinking, then there is another problem.

It is a good idea to avoid any stressful activity such as introducing new birds to the flock or bird shows during molting as the immune system may be slightly weaker than usual.

Introducing new birds

All new birds introduced to the flock should be quarantined beforehand to reduce the risk of disease. However, introducing new birds can be stressful because it will disturb the pecking order. Established flocks generally do not take kindly to new birds and until a new pecking order has been established, there will be fighting, bloodshed or even death.

If the flock has a rooster, it is not a good idea, and sometimes it is even impossible, to introduce a new rooster. Doing so can cause one or both of the roosters severe injury or death. Introducing a rooster to a flock which is made of only female birds is generally problem free. Occasionally one or two of the females may challenge the new rooster but they settle down into a pecking order very quickly. Sometimes an older rooster will tolerate a very young rooster but generally a rooster over six weeks old will not be tolerated. If you are keeping multiple roosters, the housing, the outdoor runs and the females will need to be divided between them

Chapter 9: Care and Husbandry

or the old rooster will need to be re-homed or otherwise removed. It is more common for a chicken owner to be introducing new females to the existing flock. Females of any species can be particularly aggressive so it is never a good idea to just leave the new birds with the existing flock. You should try to introduce two or more birds at a time. This means that no single bird will have the aggression of an entire flock directed solely at them. If there is more than one bird, then the aggression and bullying will be divided up between them.

One of the best ways to do this is to move all the birds into a new area but this is not always possible. Another good idea is to put the new birds into a cage or a safe enclosure next to, or near the existing flock. Doing this means that the existing birds can show the new birds the pecking order without causing any damage or injury. As a general rule, the healthy and active older bird will dominate younger birds in the pecking order. However if the older bird is not healthy or active, then the younger birds may challenge its position in the pecking order. The level of assertiveness or aggressiveness in any individual bird depends on the individual personality as well as its breed.

If caging the new birds is not possible, they can be put in with the flock after roosting. Alternatively after the existing flock is outside, the new birds can be allowed into the housing area. Regardless of which method is used to introduce new birds, the caretaker should expect there to be some fighting as a new packing order is established. Once the pecking order is in place, the fighting (?? "should stop"). If there is a rooster with the flock, he will probably step in and protect the new birds. He may even punish the aggressive birds.

If there are injured and bleeding birds, they should be removed but otherwise the flock should be allowed to sort out the pecking order on their own. The daily caretaker should watch the new birds to make sure that they are getting to the food and water sources. If the new birds remain in a corner they may need to be removed.
Old wives' tales such as spraying the birds with water or scented

Chapter 9: Care and Husbandry

products do not work and cause more stress.

Chicken bullies
Chickens are naturally bullies. They will pick on weak or injured members, often until they kill an injured bird. They will often pick on a bird that has different feathers, coloring or patterns. Birds who have top knots are often the victims of bullying by other birds and if the caretaker sees this, then the victim should be removed for its own safety. Generally flocks that have some outside time per day have very few problems with bullying. This is because they have more space which means that the chickens who are lower in the pecking order can avoid the more dominant birds. The outside space also means that the birds can spend their day scratching, dust bathing and hunting for food.

Bullying is a more common problem in chickens who do not have any outside time and are almost always confined. It is a good idea to enrich the housing of confined birds by giving them vegetables to peck at or by scattering grain throughout the house for the birds to scratch at.

If there is a bird or two in the flock which are considerably more aggressive, it may be necessary to remove them for the health, stress levels and safety of the flock as a whole.

Grooming
There are several grooming practices which are designed either for the welfare of the bird or for showing. Some chicken owners will mark their birds to allow easy identification. Permanent identification is necessary for show birds but owners of flocks of birds who look alike, may want birds to be easily identified for medication, mating or for other reasons.

One of the practices for show birds is dubbing. It is necessary for the showing of old English and modern game breeds. Dubbing involves removing the comb and wattles. This was originally done with birds who were used for cockfighting to prevent the comb and wattles from being torn during the fight. This procedure is only for

Chapter 9: Care and Husbandry

old English and modern game birds and is not necessary for any other breed. If the old English and modern game birds are not show birds, it is not recommended to dub them as the practice is painful. However, in the case of frostbite it may be necessary for health reasons.

Identifications
There are bands which can go around the leg or the wing which can be used as identifications. These bands can be metal or plastic, flat or round and they come in many different sizes. The temporary bands can be numbered or colored. There are bands for the leg which usually consist of a coil which is spread apart and placed on the leg. There are others for the wings which are plastic and can be written on. They slap over the wing at the shoulder. Temporary bands are useful for identifying birds for mating, for record-keeping and for medication.

Permanent bands can be metal or plastic and are numbered. Some supply companies will let you choose the identifying letters and numbers on the bands but generally they are sold pre-numbered. There are two types of permanent bands. Leg bands are put onto the leg of the chick and are never removed for its entire lifetime. There are also wing bands which are clamped through the wing web.

As well as bands, it is possible to microchip chickens. However to do this the owner must purchase the chips, the method of insertion and a service which will hold the information on the microchip but chickens are rarely scanned with the microchip scanner in the event that an owner must be found. However, it is still worth doing it, just in case.

Trimming the nails, wings and other feathers
Sometimes the nails of the chicken may grow to be quite long which can make walking difficult and the nails can be caught. This is usually a more common problem in caged or otherwise confined birds. Trimming the nails is a two-person job as one person will need to hold the bird while the other trims the nails with a pet nail

Chapter 9: Care and Husbandry

trimming device. There is a vein which runs about three quarters of the way up the nail which will bleed greatly if it is cut. This vein grows as the nail grows. You may be able to see the vein if there is a good light. You should only trim about a quarter of the nail at a time.

If the vein is cut, is important to put pressure on the bleeding immediately. Styptic powder should be applied. Any bleeding must be completely stopped before the bird is returned to the flock.

Some chicken owners trim the wings to prevent chickens from flying over the fencing. It is possible that some breeds may still be able to fly with trimmed wings. Chickens who have had the wings trimmed are not able to be shown.

This procedure is not permanent and will need to be repeated after every molt. This is also a two-person job. The wing should be extended and all the long flight feathers should be trimmed. If an immature feather is cut it will bleed. The bleeding feather should be pulled out. Doing this will stop the bleeding. Cutting the feathers is much better practice than pulling, which is painful.

Other feathers that should be trimmed are top knots. These fellows grow on top of the head and can often inhibit the bird's sight. If the birds can see better, they are more active and less likely to be bullied. However show birds who have trimmed top knots will be disqualified. Some breeds may develop matted feathers around the rear end or heavily feathered breeds can have so many feathers that it interferes with mating. Then feathers can be trimmed.

Chapter 10: Hatching and Incubating

It takes 21 days for a fertilized egg to develop into a chick which is big enough to survive outside the egg. This time period is known as incubation.

1) Natural Hatching

The hormones which cause broodiness or the nesting instincts are affected by the amount of daylight hours. For a hen to sit on eggs she must be laying well, in good health and have access to good quality food. Some breeds have evolved to have fewer hormones that cause broodiness. These breeds are better at producing eggs because of this. Hens who go broody stop laying eggs.

There are some breeds which are unlikely to sit on the eggs. In these breeds it is estimated that there is a less than 10% chance of the birds going broody. These breeds include Rhode Island Reds, White Rocks, Minorca, Hamburg and Leghorns.
There are breeds that may sit and are estimated to have a 50% chance of the birds going broody. These breeds include Plymouth Rocks, Old English Game, New Hampshire, Japanese and Maran. There are breeds which will sit often and it is estimated that they have a greater than 75% chance of going broody.

These breeds include Jersey Giants, Orpingtons, Silkies and Brahma. In the breeds that are most likely to sit on eggs, having the right environmental conditions and the right number of eggs will trigger broodiness. However, it is still important to remember that each bird is an individual and some will make better mothers than others.

Chapter 10: Hatching and Incubating

Encouraging broodiness
Chickens can be encouraged by their environmental conditions to go broody. The lights can be manipulated to mimic longer days. However, this should not be done in cold months unless the coop has a heating system to mimic the warmer temperatures. The first few eggs may become chilled enough to die and if conditions are very cold, the eggs that have been laid later may die also. Hens like dark nest boxes, and plenty of material should be available to them for nest building. Some chicken owners like to keep the nest boxes for hatching eggs and the nest boxes for collecting eggs in separate areas of the coop, or even enclose the broody hen to protect her. Some active breeds may bully a hen who is incubating eggs. Some broody birds will try to incubate unfertilized eggs, or rocks or anything remotely egg shaped.

If there is a rooster with broody birds, his reaction depends on his individual personality. Some roosters will lead the hen to a nest site and even stand guard for her on occasion. Other roosters may harass the broody bird and try to force her from the nest.

Adding eggs
Some chicken owners will add eggs from other birds to the nest of a broody hen. The new eggs should be as close as possible to the developmental stage of the hen's own eggs. If the sitting hen is a large breed, she should have between ten to twelve eggs in total. A bantam hen should have no more than ten to twelve bantam sized eggs and no more than six to eight large eggs. To store eggs from another hen, they need to be kept at a temperature between 45 to 65 degrees Fahrenheit or 7.2 to 18.3 degrees Celsius. The eggs need to be stored with the pointed end facing down and the larger end up. It is also a good idea to tilt the eggs daily. If the eggs are stored for more than ten days, it is probable that they will not hatch.

Some chicken owners purchase eggs to place under a broody hen. It is a good idea to wait until the bird is sitting before ordering the eggs. This may mean that it will take her a little longer to hatch the eggs. The original eggs that the bird laid will need to be

Chapter 10: Hatching and Incubating

removed. If they remain, they will hatch earlier than the new eggs. If some chicks hatch even two days before the other eggs, it is probable that the bird will abandon the eggs to mother the hatched chicks. The hen will need to be sitting firmly before any eggs are placed under her. Some people use fake eggs to make a clutch to encourage the bird to sit firmly. Once she has settled, the fake eggs can be removed and the proper eggs can be set underneath the bird. It is important to remove the fake eggs carefully and in as stress free a way as possible. The bird will probably peck, flap her wings and be vocal as you take the eggs. The new eggs need to be protected in your hand when you slide them under her. On occasion, a hen may throw a new egg out of the nest. This may happen if the egg is a different size or color to her own eggs. If this happens, the egg should be carefully put back in the nest. Some people will use chickens to hatch duck eggs using these same methods.

The sitting hen
It can be a good idea to isolate the sitting birds from the non-sitting birds in the flock. The non-sitting birds, or even the rooster, may bully and harass the sitting hen. It is even possible for a predator to take her. A sitting hen will not leave her nest and this makes her an easy target. If the hen is free range, she still needs to be protected. If possible, surround her with mesh fencing and cover the top with a board or tarp. Some birds may not mind the whole nest being carefully moved to a more secure location. Sitting birds do not require a lot of space. They need enough room to stand, stretch, flap the wings, and for the food and water bowls. Bantams need around two square foot of space and large breeds need around three square foot of space.

If it becomes necessary to move the nest, it is best to do it at night. If possible slide something carefully under the nest, with the eggs and hen inside. Some hens may fly off the nest and will need to be caught and moved with the eggs. If the bird is not caught she will not know where the eggs have gone. The bird should then be confined with the nest. Usually by morning the bird will be perfectly happy with the new nesting location, but ensure that she

Chapter 10: Hatching and Incubating

cannot get to the original location. Sometimes a bird will go back to the first nesting site and abandon the eggs. If this needs to be done during daylight, the nest must be set up beforehand. The hen and eggs should be moved quickly into the new darkened location and then left alone.

While hens cannot carry the eggs, they may roll them back into the nest if they have accidentally come out. Some chicken owners mark an egg which is outside the nest before putting it back in. if the egg is outside of the nest again, then the hen may have decided that there is something wrong with it, or some birds can be quite clumsy when nesting. If the egg comes out of the nest more than three times, it should be discarded. If possible, handling the eggs should be avoided and they should not be cleaned.

Sitting hens do not eat or drink often. A sitting hen needs less food and water than normal. This is because she isn't particularly active and eating a lot of food means that she will have to leave the nest more often. The food and water bowls should be placed a short distance from the hen to encourage her to get up every so often. If the pen around the nest gets very dirty it can be cleaned but otherwise, a sitting hen can be left alone.

Mother and chicks
It takes around thirty six hours for a chick to hatch. The hen will stay on the nest for around two days after the first chick hatches. The chicken owner may hear the chick or see a head coming from under the hen or only see bits of eggshell outside the nest. After two days the hen will leave the nest to lead the chicks to food and water. Some chicken owners like to raise the chicks themselves in a brooder and collect the chicks around three days after hatching. Waiting for three days means that any late hatching eggs still have a chance to hatch. The first few days of a chick's life are spent mostly under the hen. It is important to keep the area quiet and not to handle the chicks until the hen is a little more relaxed and the chicks are a little older. Do not allow children or adult visitors to make a lot of noise near the mother and chicks.

Chapter 10: Hatching and Incubating

The chicks should be given a chick starter feed in shallow bowls. Water should be given in a container with a narrow opening. Do not leave an open container of water near chicks. As they grow they become more inquisitive and can fall into the water and drown. The mother will show them how to eat and drink. The chicks will spend quite a bit of time under the mother particularly if they are cold or scared. If the temperature is cold, it is a good idea to supply a heat lamp and some warm bedding material. The area does need to be kept dry as chicks can get wet and chilled which can lead to death.

It is possible to separate the chicks from the hen at any time but it is best to wait until they are fully feathered which is around four to six weeks. Again, if the temperatures are cold they will need a heat lamp after separation, but if the temperature is fine then they should be alright without one. Chicks can be allowed out at this time with their mother but they are vulnerable to attack from predators and even other birds. It is a good idea to introduce fully feathered chicks to the flock by putting them and their mother in with the flock at roosting time. If they are not wounded the next day, they can be left with the flock but if they are wounded, they need to be removed from the flock. Young roosters should be housed separately if there is an existing rooster in the flock.

2) Artificial Hatching

There are several reasons for artificial hatching: some hens won't sit on eggs, some chicken owners find it easier to incubate or the eggs may be too large to hatch all of them under a hen. The first recorded incubation method was to heat rotted manure and put the eggs in it. The Egyptians used a round building with a fire on the bottom. The eggs were put in a basket which sat on top of an inverted cone that was partially covered in ash. In ancient Greece, it was recorded that women tried to incubate eggs themselves by keeping them under their clothes, close to the chest. The first mechanical incubator was invented in 1749 and the first commercial machine was made in 1881.

Chapter 10: Hatching and Incubating

There are many incubators available for purchase. Before purchasing, it is important to consider the budget, how often it will be used, how many eggs will be hatched at a time, if any other birds will be hatched in the incubator, for example ducks, and how involved you want to be. Some incubators come with windows so the caretaker can observe the hatching. This is also useful if there are children who want to see the chicks hatching. If incubation is not going to be a regular occurrence, it is more cost effective to buy a cheaper model or a second hand incubator. If you plan to incubate often, it is a good idea to buy a better incubator. If there will be ducks or other poultry eggs hatching in it, then it will need to be able to accommodate the larger eggs of these birds. Most incubators are electric, but gas ones exist, and are meant to be in a heated room.

Incubators
Still air incubators are the cheapest type of incubator. They are made of Styrofoam or plastic and come in a variety of sizes to accommodate from 4 eggs to 36 eggs. They can have windows or clear tops for observation.

Still air incubators work by taking in and moving air through while it is heated. Some models have fans to move the air, while in others the air is moved by the process of heating it as warm air rises. There is usually a reservoir at the bottom and the caretaker adds water to provide the humidity. Some models have egg turners, but if not, the eggs will need to be turned by hand. Still air incubators need very careful attention on a daily basis. They will provide a good hatch as long as the instructions are followed closely and attention is given.

Forced air incubators move heated air by a fan system. They are more expensive than still air incubators but they do give a better hatch. This is because still air incubators can have hot and cold spots but forced air incubators tend to give a more even distribution of heated air. They can have automatic humidifiers, automatic egg turners, warning buzzers and observation windows. The extras like warning buzzers will depend on the cost of the

Chapter 10: Hatching and Incubating

model. The come in different sizes, usually accommodating 12 to 50 eggs. Most backyard chicken keeper prefer this type of incubator. They do still need attention but not as much as the still air type.

Cabinet style incubators are large units with several shelves so they can hatch eggs that are at different stages of development. They use forced air to incubate the eggs and have automatic humidifiers and automatic egg turners but they do not usually have observation windows. They tend to be very expensive unless bought second hand.

Automatic egg turners turn the eggs consistently and gently which can be better than turning by hand. Some chicken owners find that an incubator with an automatic egg turner increases the chances of a good hatch. They have to be turned off three days before hatching.

Not included extras
There are some items which are very useful to have for incubating but that are not included when purchasing an incubator.
A thermometer should be placed near the top of the eggs. It can be put on a stand or hung. However, it shouldn't touch the eggs or the walls. The display should be large enough to be read without having to open the incubator. A more expensive option is a probe or sensor which is kept in the incubator and transmits the temperature reading to a device outside. It is important to monitor the temperature as the proper temperature is crucial to the hatching.

A hygrometer measures the humidity. Humidity is also extremely important for hatching. Many incubators have built in hygrometers and some have automatic humidifiers. Many of the probe and sensor thermometers also measure the humidity.

The new incubator
After purchasing and receiving the new incubator, the instructions must be carefully read and stored. The incubator needs to be near an electrical socket in a room that is heated to at least 60 degrees Fahrenheit or 15.6 degrees Celsius. It should be away from

Chapter 10: Hatching and Incubating

windows, heating vents, doors and should be somewhere safe where it cannot be knocked or shaken. It should be out of the sight and, if possible, hearing of children and pets. Children tend to open the incubator too often and handle the eggs or touch the controls. Pets can hear hatching and newly hatched chicks and may attempt to get at them which can damage both the incubator and the eggs. The incubator needs to be running for at least 24 hours before any eggs are put inside it. This is to ensure that it is working correctly.

Cleaning the incubator
Incubators need to be cleaned before every use, even the first use. Any debris should be removed and then the incubator should be washed in hot soapy water and then rinsed. It is important not to submerse any parts in water before checking that it is safe to do so. The screens that the eggs sit on and the egg turning racks also need to be washed and rinsed. If possible, allow the incubator and parts to dry in the sun but if not, it can be dried with clean paper towels. Disinfectants and cleaning solutions should not be used as the residue can harm the developing chicks by passing through the shell.

Temperature
The temperature must be correct for the eggs to hatch. In a still air incubator, the temperature should be 102 degrees Fahrenheit or 38.9 degrees Celsius. In most other incubators the temperature should be 100 degrees Fahrenheit or 37.8 degrees Celsius. The instruction manual can help provide information on the correct temperature for each brand and model of incubator. The temperature should be set correctly before the eggs are added to the incubator.
The temperature inside can be affected by opening the incubator and how often it is opened, the external temperatures and the development of the eggs. Most incubators have a thermostat which should automatically adjust the temperature to the correct levels. However, it is a good idea to check the thermometer often and adjust the thermostat as needed.
A short period of cool air, for example if the eggs are turned by

Chapter 10: Hatching and Incubating

hand, shouldn't harm the eggs unless it happens too often. However a short period of temperatures of 104 degrees Fahrenheit or 40 degrees Celsius or above can kill most, if not all, of the developing chicks.

As the eggs get close to hatching, they will produce some heat which can raise the temperature in the incubator. It is important to monitor very closely and adjust the temperature when the eggs get close to hatching. It is also important not to open the door during hatching. Doing this can cool and kill the chicks.

Humidity

The humidity in the incubator must also be correct. It should be 55 per cent for the first nineteen days and 65 to 70 per cent for the last two days. Humidity can be increased by adding water to a reservoir in the incubator. In still air incubators this is a pan under the screen that the eggs sit on, but other types can have other reservoir systems. The water should be heated to the temperature of the incubator before adding it to the reservoir. If the eggs seem wet or there is dripping water, then the humidity is too high and this can kill the chicks. If this happens, then more ventilation is needed to reduce the humidity, but it is important to monitor the temperature to ensure it does not drop too low.

Ventilation

Chicks will absorb oxygen through the eggshell before they hatch. All incubators must have a system for allowing stale air to leave the incubator and for fresh air to enter. In still air incubators this is through small openings which can be open and closed manually, other incubators use fan systems. As the chicks grow, they will need more oxygen so the ventilation may need to be increased. It can be difficult to tell if the ventilation levels are correct but the instruction manual that came with the incubator will have instructions on how to adjust the ventilation which will be appropriate for that particular system. However, it is important to increase the ventilation on the eighteenth day of incubation. The temperature and humidity should be adjusted also, if doing this causes their levels to fall.

Chapter 10: Hatching and Incubating

Turning eggs

It is widely thought that the best way of turning eggs is to turn two to three times per day for the first eighteen days. Turning prevents the chicks from attaching to the membranes and shell. Automatic egg turners will do this but if this needs to be done by hand, it should be done as gently and quickly as possible so the eggs do not get too cold. If the incubator has egg racks, the eggs should be put in with the small end down. If the incubator has no egg racks, the eggs should be laid on their sides. It is important to wash your hands before touching the eggs as any oils or bacteria on your hands can affect the eggs. It is also important to wash your hands after handling eggs. On the eighteenth day, stop turning the eggs or turn off the automatic egg turner. The chicks get into hatching position and moving them now can alter the position which means that they would have to get back into position.

Hatching

The humidity need to be increased to 65 - 70 per cent on the eighteenth day of incubation. The ventilation may also need to be increased but it is important to refer to the incubator's instructions to see if this is necessary. The brooder should be set up and warmed on the 20th day so it is ready for the chicks. The hatching process can take time but the eggs should hatch within eighteen hours of each other. It is important to leave the door of the incubator closed until the chicks are hatched and dry. Every six hours, the chicks who have hatched and are dry and fluffy can be removed and put in the brooder. If there are eggs which have not hatched after eighteen hours, they can be left for a further twenty four hours. After this, it is unlikely that they will hatch and can be examined for signs of pipping or thrown out.

Helping hatch

Some chicks can struggle to hatch. It is important to allow plenty of time for a chick to hatch by itself before intervening but on occasion it may become necessary to do so. Most chicken owners believe that a chick who needs help to hatch will die anyway or be a weak unhealthy bird. If you do decide to help a chick hatch,

Chapter 10: Hatching and Incubating

it must be done slowly and carefully. There should be a clean, padded and warm surface. A small pair of scissors and a pair of tweezers should be sterilized by boiling or with rubbing alcohol, and there should be warm, clean water close by. With the scissors and tweezers, the pieces of shell can be carefully picked away from the membrane. Care must be taken not to pierce the membrane which has blood veins. Piercing the vein will cause it to bleed which can weaken or even kill the chick. If this happens the chick needs to go back into the incubator until the bleeding stops. After an hour when the bleeding has stopped and if the chick is still not out of the egg, you can try again.

When picking off the shell, you should work in circles around the larger end of the egg like the chick would. Extra care should be taken if the chick tried to hatch at the smaller end of the egg, and it is very important not to cut the chick. If the head and neck of the chick is free from eggshell, it should become active and wiggle out the rest of the way. The remaining membrane should be moistened with warm, clean water and the chick should be put back into the incubator with some shell still attached. If the chick is not up and walking within an hour, unfortunately, it probably isn't going to survive.

Problems in hatching
There are some common problems in hatching. If the eggs hatch early, there are two possible explanations. The temperature may have been too high, or the caretaker counted the days incorrectly. If the eggs hatch late, the temperature was too low or the caretaker counted the days incorrectly.
If the eggs hatch over a long time period, the eggs may have been stored incorrectly. There may have been hot and cold spots in the incubator.
If the eggs have not hatched by day 22, open some. If there is no embryo then the egg was either too old to incubate or it was never fertilized. If the embryo started forming but died, it could be due to incorrect temperature, incorrect humidity, incorrect ventilation, bacterial contamination, disease, not being turned enough or being handled too roughly.

If there are living embryos in the eggs, give the unopened eggs more time to hatch.

If the hatched chicks have a sticky goo on them, the humidity may have been too high, the ventilation may have been inadequate, the temperature may have been too low or it may be a symptom of an inherited condition.
Some chicks hatch crippled or malformed. this can be due to a slightly high incubation temperature, disease, chemical contamination in the incubator, or not turning the eggs enough. If the legs are crippled or malformed, it may be due to hatching on a slippery surface.
If the chicks have a mushy, large or bloody navel area, then it could be due to the temperature being slightly too low, the humidity being too high or it may be due to Omphalitis which is caused by bacteria. Therefore, it is important for the chicks to hatch on a dry and clean surface.

3) Brooders

Chicks need to be kept warm for the first few weeks. Without warmth they will stop eating and drinking and may die. This is naturally done by a hen, but when the eggs are hatched in an incubator, or if the chicken owner wants the hen to begin producing eggs as quickly as possible, then the chicks must go into a brooder. A brooder is an enclosed space with a heat source which keeps the chicks warm and protected. Essentially, it takes over the job from the hen. The chicks need to be moved directly from the incubator to the brooder and kept there for about four weeks. They may need longer in cold weather.

However, it is important to take extra care in hot weather as chicks can over heat. Anything above 100 degrees Fahrenheit or 37.8 degrees Celsius is too warm. Average size chicks need 6 square inches per chick in the brooder. The brooder needs to be at least 18 inches deep. If the heat source is an overhead heat lamp, it will need to be adjusted as the chicks grow so as to ensure that it doesn't actually touch the chicks. There should be a cover for

Chapter 10: Hatching and Incubating

the brooder to prevent chicks from escaping. The chicks also need to be able to move around the brooder to get to a warm spot when they are cold or a cool spot when they are warm. A heat lamp should be placed at one end of a rectangle brooder which allows the other end to be cool. In square or round brooders, the heat lamp should be in the middle. If the heat source is powered by anything other than electric, it is imperative to put a carbon monoxide detector nearby.

Temperature
The temperature of the brooder for the first week need to be at 95 degrees Fahrenheit or 35 degrees Celsius. The temperature should be taken at the height of a chick's back which is around two inches from the floor of the brooder. Each week, the temperature should be lowered by 5 degrees until it reaches 70 degrees Fahrenheit or 20 degrees Celsius. If the outside temperature goes below 60 degrees Fahrenheit or 15.6 degrees Celsius at night, then the brooder should be kept at 60 degrees Fahrenheit (15.6 degrees Celsius).
Gas or propane powered brooders will usually have a thermostat. If a heat lamp is the heat source, then the brooder will need a good non mercury thermometer to keep note of the temperature levels. There are specialist brooder thermometers available but any thermometer will do. The temperature should be checked often for the first few days. Doing this can help establish what change the outside temperature has on the brooder. If the temperature is too high, it can be adjusted by increasing ventilation, changing the position of the heat lamp or changing the size or wattage of the bulb. Infrared lamps may not be correctly measurable on a thermometer as they heat the chicks not the air. Watch the chicks carefully if using an infrared lamp.

Some chicken owners hang two different size bulbs in the brooder so they can be switched on or off if there are big changes in day and night temperatures.
Most brooders have solid sides which help retain heat. If the temperature continuously gets too hot, it may be a good idea to drill holes, a few inches from the bottom, in the sides of the

Chapter 10: Hatching and Incubating

brooder. These will draw in cool air as the hot air rises. The holes need to be small enough that the chicks cannot escape.

Another way of checking the temperature of a brooder is to look at the behavior of the chicks in it. If they are walking, eating and drinking and some are sleeping near the heat source, then the temperature is probably fine. If they are panting with their beaks open, drinking lots but not really eating, are spread at the coolest spot in the breeder and as far away from the heat source as they can get, then it is too warm. If they are huddled near the heat source, cheeping loudly and not really eating, then they are too cold. If you notice either of these behaviors, correct the temperature because too much cold or too much heat can kill the chicks.

Lighting
If the heat source of the brooder is a bulb or heat lamp, then it may not be necessary to have any more lighting. If the heat source includes red bulbs and infrared bulbs then it may be a good idea to have lighting. Any additional lighting must be far enough away from the brooder so that it doesn't affect the temperature. The lights should be kept on for around 12 hours per day for pet and laying chicks, but for broilers, the lights need to be on 24 hours per day. If the chicks are moving into housing that gets dark when the lights go off, they will need to be prepared for this by using a dim light or a night light.

Bedding
The brooder will need some bedding. Do not use newspaper or any kind of paper, cardboard or plastic as bedding. They become slippery when they are wet and can affect the legs of the chicks. Do not use soil, vermiculite, perlite, cedar shavings, cat litter, hay, straw, leaves or cotton batting. Hay, straw and leaves can contain harmful substances and also get slippery and moldy when wet. Do not use shavings from unknown wood or hardwood. Also, shavings can develop mold.

Many chicken owners prefer to use pine shavings. Clean sand, coarse sawdust, and chick grit can also be used

The bedding should be changed completely when it is damp and

Chapter 10: Hatching and Incubating

smelly. If it is dry but dirty, then a fresh layer can be added. However a complete bedding change should happen before the bedding is too deep. The chicks will need to be removed for this and placed in a box where they will be safe. If you use a disinfectant, then the brooder will need to be thoroughly rinsed and dried before putting in new bedding and the chicks.

The brooder should be cleaned thoroughly when the chicks are re-housed, and before a new batch of chicks use it. It will need to be disinfected with 1 part bleach to 4 parts water, rinsed and dried in the sun.

Commercial brooders
Commercial brooders are available but they are expensive. The cost of shipping a commercial brooder can be as much as the brooder itself. It is a good idea to check local advertisements for new and second hand brooders which could be collected rather than shipped. One type of commercial brooder is the battery brooder. It consists of small cages stacked on top of each other. However, the chicks do not have a lot of head room and will need to be moved in a short time when they grow too big for it.

Other types of commercial brooder will consist of a heat source which is enclosed in a hover or metal ring. This unit is placed into a larger confined area which needs to be weather proof.

Making a brooder
Many chicken owners make their own brooders as it is much cheaper than buying one. It needs to be easy to move, easy to clean, strong enough to keep out predators, large enough for all the chicks, and not be able to be melted by the heat source. It needs to be in a dry building with an electric supply. It is not a good idea to keep it inside the house as the chicks smell, raise dust and are a source of salmonella bacteria. It is also a fire hazard in the house. Some chicken owners like the brooder to be on the floor while others prefer them to be elevated. If you put yours on the floor put some cardboard, or newspapers under it to protect it from the cold floor. The top on the brooder must be strong and be able to provide ventilation. The electric cord from the heat source will need to come out from either the top or a

corner.

The body of the brooder can be made from wood, but the wood needs to be fairly thick to provide insulation. It can have a bottom or it can be set directly on the floor or on a tray. Wire mesh can be used to make the top. Wood, plexi-glass or glass can be used to cover some of the top which will keep the heat in but still allow for ventilation. In cold temperatures, a brooder with solid sides is best but in hot temperatures, it is a good idea to make one or two of the sides from mesh to aid ventilation and keep the chicks from overheating.

The body can also be made from a stock tank, which is a large tank used to water livestock. These are made from metal or heavy duty resin and come in many different sizes. They are oval or round and long lasting. They are expensive, but even a leaking tank will make an excellent brooder.

A child's swimming pool can also be used as a brooder but not the inflatable type. The strong plastic or metal sided ones can be used. If you use a metal one, it is only the sides that are needed for making the brooder.

Plastic storage containers can be used but they may melt if the heat source is too close.

Do not use cardboard. It will disintegrate when wet. It is hard to clean and it may catch fire. Do not use containers from toxic materials like pesticides. Some containers emit the chemical as a gas, even after washing.

To heat the brooder remember that chicks prefer an overhead heat source and that they prefer to have some light with the heat. Do not set the brooder on a heating pad as floor heat is not a good way to keep chicks warm.

Some chicken owners like to use a reflector light. It needs to have a ceramic socket and a UL listed tag and a ring on the back so it can be hung overhead. Some reflector lights have a guard on the front to prevent the bulb from touching the bedding if the light falls. Try to avoid plastic socket reflector lights as the brooder may need a high wattage bulb and they can melt the plastic socket.

Chapter 10: Hatching and Incubating

There should be a tag or an embossing to tell you the maximum wattage for the socket.

If the brooder is in a warm area, it may be possible to use a regular bulb. Do not use fluorescent bulbs as they give no heat. If the brooder is in colder temperatures then it will be necessary to use a heat bulb or reflector bulb. Heat bulbs have two wavelength variations - infrared and regular light. The infrared bulbs can be difficult to use as the heat from them does not measure well on a thermometer, which makes it difficult to regulate the heat in the brooder.

The light of a regular bulb may seem strong but the chicks do not mind. The reflector bulbs focus the light downwards, which means that other areas of the brooder are dimmer.

The number and wattage of the bulbs is dependent on the temperature of the room, the size of the brooder, the material of the brooder and the number of chicks in it. You may need to experiment to find out which bulb works best for your brooder. It is advisable do this before the chicks have hatched. Remember that it is not the entire brooder that needs to be heated, only enough space for all the chicks to sit comfortably without being on top of each other. If you need to have more than one lamp in the brooder then you can experiment with the combination of wattages as well, but they should be close together so that there is still a warmer area and a cooler area. When buying the bulbs it is a good idea to buy more than one, as bulbs can fail. This means that there will be a back up bulb if this happens. Also buy another smaller bulb so that if the chicks are too hot, the smaller bulb can be a cooler replacement. It can also be used when the chicks are bigger and do not need as much heat.

The heat lamps should be suspended so as to provide the heat from overhead. If the brooder is square or round, then the lamp should be in the middle but if the brooder is a rectangle or oval, the heat lamp should hang at one end of it. The lamp should be raised or lowered to adjust the temperature. So do not suspend the light by the cord, as it can pull out and cause the lamp to fall. Use a chain or wire from the ring on the back of a reflector. Start with a distance of about a foot from the floor of the brooder. If this is incorrect then raise or lower it as needed. The lamp should never touch the chicks. If the bulb needs to be raised above the top of the brooder, replace it with a lower wattage. If the bulb needs to be lowered too close to the chicks, then replace it with a higher wattage bulb. As the chicks grow they will need less heat so the bulb can be raised or replaced with a lower wattage bulb.

Safety
Heat lamps and other heat sources can cause fire so extreme care must be taken.
Always use UL (not sure if this is just a US term?) approved items. Never go over the maximum wattage of a socket. Always check cords and do not use cords that are frayed or damaged. Use proper extension cords if needed, but only use outdoor appropriate cords for outdoor areas. Keep cords out of wet areas and areas with high foot traffic. Never suspend a light by its cord. Leave the guards on the reflector. Keep heat bulbs away from flammable material and material which can melt. Keep the water dishes away from the heat lamps. Keep the cords out of the brooders and away from access by other animals. If the heat source is gas or propane, it is very important that the ventilation is good. Use a carbon monoxide detector for gas and propane brooders. Make sure any combustible material is not touching a heat source.

4) Raising Chicks

Chicks do not need to eat or drink for a day or two after hatching. They still have the remaining egg yolk which will sustain them. This is so the whole clutch has enough time to hatch. After a day or two the hen will lead them to food and water. If they were hatched in an incubator, then food and water should be offered when they are dry and walking.

Chapter 10: Hatching and Incubating

Starter feed
Chicks can eat adult chicken feed, bread crumbs and other food stuffs but they do not do well on these feeds. Chick feed is formulated and sized for chicks which makes it the best choice as a feed. Chicks are quick growing and need a high protein feed. Broiler chicks particularly must have a high protein diet or they may develop leg problems. The protein level should be a minimum of 22 per cent. If there is not enough protein in the feed, the legs can become twisted and weak and the wings can become distorted. For a pet or laying breed, a feed with 20 per cent protein can be given but if there are any meat birds in the flock, 22 per cent protein must be given to all. Lower protein feed can be given to the other chicks after the meat birds are separated. Most commercial feeds do not need added grit, but if commercial feed is not given, chick grit must be added. It is possible to use canary or parakeet grit if chick grit cannot be sourced.

Some chicken owners give the chicks medicated feed. Medicated feed includes antibiotics, parasite control and medication that help with stress related illnesses. Meat breeds need to be off medicated feed for a number of weeks before butchering. Some chicken owners use medicated feed with pet and laying breeds until the chicks are able to eat adult feed. As an alternative to medicated feed, an anti-stress formula can be added to the water. However, nothing should be added to the water of chicks on medicated feed.

Food and water containers
The food bowls for chicks need to be shallow for the first few weeks. As the chicks grow, the feed containers should get larger. You can use either several feed containers or one large enough to feed all the chicks at the same time. Meat chicks need to have a constant supply of food. Other breeds do not need the same constant supply but if they crowd newly filled feed bowls or act extremely hungry, then they are not getting enough feed.
Water should always be accessible for the chicks. There are waterers available for chicks which have shallow and narrow openings. If you are using any other container, it must not be more than a few inches deep as chicks can drown in deeper

Chapter 10: Hatching and Incubating

containers. It is important to prevent the chicks from walking or perching on the container. Marbles and stones can be added to reduce the open surface of an open container. The area where the waterer is should be always kept clean. The area around it may be wet and bedding may become kicked into the water. Some chicken owners put the waterer and feed bowls on a tray so as to contain the mess and keep bedding and feed from contaminating the water. The water should be as far away from the heat source as possible. Some chicken owners advise adding a teaspoon of sugar, some add sports drink or a special mix to the water. This is usually unnecessary, but it may help chicks who are particularly weak.

In the brooder
For the first day or two, the bedding should be covered with textured paper towel or rough paper. There should also be a large tray or lid with feed scattered on it on top of the paper. Doing this encourages the chicks to eat. The normal dishes should also be in the brooder. The chicks may try to eat the bedding and covering it will prevent this. If the chicks were shipped, each chick should be taken out singly and its beak dipped in the water to encourage it to drink as it may be slightly dehydrated. Do not hold the beak in the water. If there is a very weak chick, you should try to get some warm water into the beak and then leave it under the heat source. While the chicks should be checked often during the first few days, they should not be disturbed. After a day or two and if the chicks are eating properly, the covering paper can be removed.

Disease prevention
It is important to reduce the risk of the chicks catching disease as much as possible. Keep the chicks away from adult birds and older chicks. Do not mix chicks bought from different sources. Wash your hands between caring for different groups and between the older chicks and adults. Do not interchange the feed containers and waterers. If possible mark them to identify which container is for which brooder. Keep the area and containers clean. Keep an eye on the birds for signs of disease and illness and remove and isolate birds who appear to be ill.

Chapter 10: Hatching and Incubating

One month old
At a month old, as long as the chicks are fully feathered, they can leave the brooder. They may still need a heat lamp if the weather is cool. Bantam and slow growing breeds may need longer in the brooder. At this age, the chicks will need at least 2 square feet of space. They can go outside if it is warm and dry but will need to be observed and protected from predators. They are not old enough to free range yet.

Six - eighteen weeks
Meat birds at this age should be switched to grower or finisher feed. Pets and laying breeds can be fed a grower feed of 16 per cent protein. They can roost at this age and should have roosts available for them. The roost should be about a foot or two from the ground. Meat breeds do not roost.
At eighteen weeks, pullets that are intended for laying should be switched to a 16 per cent protein layers mix. It should have calcium and other supplements and nutrients included. If the birds are a low egg producing or slow maturing breed, the layers mix can be fed when they actually start to lay.

Adulthood
Chicks reach maturity at 18 to 25 weeks. They can be moved into the adult flock. This does need to be done carefully and with close observation. A male will crow, and once this happens he is capable of fertilizing eggs. A female may pretend to nest so it is important that pullets have access to nest boxes from 18 weeks old. This pretend nesting is believed to encourage good egg laying habits later in life.

Children
Children can be very curious and will want to see and touch the chicks. They need to be supervised and taught how to hold the bird gently and correctly. Older children may be able to be involved in the care of the birds. Adults should always lift a chick before allowing a child to hold it. The chick should never be squeezed. Children should also be taught not to make noise when near the chicks as it is very stressful to the chicks.

Chapter 11: Behavior

The behavior of the chicken can provide some indication if there is a problem. Abnormal behaviors will show that there is something wrong.

1) Behaviors of a Happy Chicken

Happy chickens will scratch the ground. They will groom, fluff their feathers and show their individual personality. They will roost and nest. Hens will go broody, depending on the breed. They will be fairly curious. They will move freely through the environment. They can be quite talkative and will cluck to each other. They will flap and stretch their wings. They will forage.

Despite popular belief, chickens, and birds in general, are quite smart. Their brains, while small, are different to the brains of mammals. They can understand counting and can be trained by reward to count items. Mammals who do this are trained to respond to signals and commands from a person, but birds seem to understand the concepts behind counting. Birds are capable of deception. They will deceive other birds and mammals which implies that they understand that actions have outcomes and consequences. Their large field of vision helps to detect predators. If they spot a predator, they quickly assess the action with the best possible outcome and will freeze or hide accordingly. They are capable of assessing differences between, for example, different dogs and recognizing which dog is a threat and which is a non threatening presence.

Noises
Chickens can be quite vocal and there is a range of noise that they will make. First it is important to look at how they process

Chapter 11: Behavior

information. They communicate with each other almost all the time. Some noises are warnings to the flock of predators, others are conversation and others still are fear noises. The crowing of a rooster is a territorial noise. Roosters will crow throughout the day, but it is only roosters who have reached sexual maturity who can produce this noise. The sound of the crow depends on the individual rooster.

The cackling noise is made immediately after egg laying. Often, the other hens join in with the hen who has laid and they can make this noise for a few minutes. It is believed that this noise is either relief of laying or pride in her egg.
Both sexes make a clucking or a chucking noise. This noise has been described as similar to a group of people having a conversation. This noise can happen at any time.
Some roosters will call the hens to a food source. They make a 'perp-perp' noise to do this. This is the same noise that mothers make to call their chicks to food.

Rebel yelling is the noise chickens make when there is a threat from a predator. The whole flock will hide after one bird has made this noise.
Chickens can make a growling sound but it is most often heard from hens who are sitting on eggs. The growl is a warning not to disturb the bird and she may peck and attack if the warning is ignored.

Squawking is a fear noise. This is the noise a bird makes when it is startled. The rest of the flock may run when they hear this noise or they may come closer.
Some birds make a purr noise when they're happy and if there are two roosters in a small space then there will be aggressive noises as they will fight.
There are other noises as well, but these are the most common.

Food behavior
As chickens have few taste buds, they will eat anything that comes in front of them. If it looks remotely like food, they will

Chapter 11: Behavior

eat it. Chicken owners need to be vigilant in ensuring that things that are bad for them are kept away from them. They eat insects, worms, vegetation, seeds and meat. They will comb through the fecal matter of other animals and find edible bits. They will turn up compost heaps looking for bugs.

They will also eat grit and small stones which go into the gizzard and aid digestion. Free range birds get enough grit and stones as they are outside with plenty of access to it. Indoor chickens may need a grit supplement provided to them. Chickens will hunt for food. Even indoor chickens will go through the motions of hunting. Almost all chickens are good at and enjoy hunting for food morsels. There are a few who are not: heavy broiler meat birds are not good and hunting nor do they enjoy it. They much prefer to sit at a feeder and eat high energy high protein feed. Chickens do not eat at night time or if they are in an unlit house.

Sleep
Chickens sleep from dusk to dawn. If there is total darkness chickens will go into a dazed trance like behavior which makes them easy prey for predators. Chicken prefer to sleep on a perch as it gives more protection from predators. They like to roost in the same spot each night. This means that free range birds generally return to the coop at night. When roosting, the foot locks around the perch and stays in that locked position until morning. This is an unconscious action for the bird and it ensures that they will not fall off during the night. In the morning they have to make a conscious effort to unlock the foot muscles.

Social behavior
Chickens are social birds. They thrive in a flock. Each flock has a pecking order among the hens. If there are two or more roosters in the flock, they will establish their own pecking order.. A flock of roosters without hens will have small fights which are generally easily resolved. Two or more roosters with hens will fight more intensely. They will cause damage to each other and on occasion this can result in death.
The rooster is the most dominant chicken in the flock. If he eats

with the hens, they will not have any dominance fights and all birds will eat peacefully. If the hens are fighting, the rooster may step in to stop this. He can be younger than his hens. If he is sexually mature then he is the most dominant chicken.

Dust bathing
Chickens will dust bathe in a dry substrate. If there is loose soil, litter or dust they will hollow out enough space to lie down in. Then they throw the soil on the feathers and shake to remove it again. Doing this helps control parasites. If necessary, a medicated bath can be used to treat parasites. The birds will treat the medicated bath the same as other substrates. They will only dust bathe in dry substrates, never in wet.

2) Abnormal Behavior

When considering abnormal behavior in chickens, it is important to remember that their environment plays an enormous part in their behaviors. A hen who is in the wrong or an abnormal environment will be unhappy and can develop some strange behaviors and even some painful and dangerous ones. Chickens from a battery hen rescue often exhibit abnormal behaviors.

There are methods of relieving the extent of the behaviors but they may be too deeply rooted to be fully changed. There are many behaviors which would be classified as abnormal. Most of these are found in all species of domestic bird, not just chickens, for example farm birds like turkeys and chickens and to pet birds like parrots and canaries. Abnormal behaviors include feather pecking, cannibalism, vent pecking, toe pecking, feather plucking, polydipsia, sham or "vacuum" dust bathing and chronic egg laying.

Feather pecking
Feather pecking is an abnormal behavior commonly found in chickens. This is when one chicken will repeatedly peck at the feathers of another. This can be gentle and severe. Chickens will feather peck at other chickens routinely but this is to investigate,

Chapter 11: Behavior

and the pecking is gentle. This feather pecking level is not problematic. The feathers of the bird being pecked are barely disturbed and there is no pain. The second, severe, level is painful. The feathers are not pecked at gently but rather are grasped and pulled. This can sometimes mean that the feathers are actually pulled forcibly out of the bird. This can cause skin trauma and bleeding.

Feather pecking is thought to develop from a lack of ground pecking. The normal behavior of a chicken is to peck and forage on the ground and chickens are not allowed to do this can develop feather pecking as an alternative. Sometimes the removed feathers are eaten. Feather eating is related to feather pecking but the motivations for each are different. Feather eating can provide some help in digestion.

Feather pecking begins early and most afflicted hens will show signs of it at around 16 - 20 weeks old. It is rare for feather pecking to develop after 40 weeks old. There is also a pattern of progress of feather pecking. It begins with the rump area and the tail feathers and then moves to the neck, wings and back. It is unclear whether there is any link between gentle and severe feather pecking.

There are some things that may help reduce feather pecking, such as ad lib feeding, the type of feeder and waterer, the breed, not adding new birds to the flock delaying egg laying, and allowing greater access to outdoor areas.

Beak trimming is also used to control feather pecking. This is sometimes referred to as debeaking but the term is inaccurate. One to two thirds of the beak is trimmed by using a blade or an infra red beam. There are many concerns over this method. The beak contains nerves and beak trimming cuts these nerves. Doing this can cause abnormal nerve regeneration. This abnormal nerve regeneration can be similar to that in human amputees which cause phantom pains in the missing limb. This could suggest that chickens who have undergone beak trimming may also feel phantom pain in the amputated part of the beak. There is also some evidence that beak trimming can impair the chicken's ability to determine direction. It is believed that the beak plays a large part in magneto-reception. This means that the beak detects the magnetic field of the earth and this helps the bird navigate its environment. Beak trimming also leaves the bird unable to groom itself as well as a full beaked bird. A bird who cannot groom properly will be unable to remove external parasites properly and will have a greater number of them than a bird who can groom properly. The Farm Animal Welfare Council in the United Kingdom advocates beak tipping as an alternative to beak trimming. Beak tipping means that the sharp point of the beak is blunted which would not cause as much damage if feather pecking was a problem. This procedure has been banned in Switzerland.

An alternative method of controlling feather pecking is light manipulation. This means that the intensity of the light is reduced. The lower light means that the birds cannot see each other as easily, which can reduce the number of incidents of aggression and stress related behaviors. The disadvantages of this are that it also becomes more difficult for humans to inspect the birds in a housing environment for damage and blood. Also, hens prefer to eat in a brightly lit area. Instant light manipulation can be a risk factor in feather pecking and other abnormal behaviors. Light should be timed to mimic natural outdoor light changes. The light should change gradually and follow a dusk to dawn pattern. This means that the birds can anticipate the changes.

Some chicken keepers use blinders to prevent feather pecking and other abnormal behaviors. Blinders are plastic, neoprene or metal pieces which are attached to the beak to block the vision. There are two methods of keeping the blinders in place - a clip into the nostrils or a pin through the nasal septum. Some have a small hole to allow restricted forward vision. They are usually brightly colored which means that it is easy to see any birds who have lost the device. There are also spectacles which allow vision but the colored lenses in them means that the colors seen by the birds are altered. This makes it harder for the bird to see and identify blood. The use of these devices is illegal in the United Kingdom. There are also pin-less blinders but these can cause feeding problems, increased resting, reduced activity and stereotypies.

Cannibalism
Cannibalism is when one bird pecks at another bird and eats the flesh. It can cause fatalities. Chickens are omnivores and will eat insects, small mice, small lizards or other meats. They generally follow a herbivore diet when they reach adulthood. However, other behaviors such as feather pecking can cause bleeding which can encourage cannibalistic behaviors. It is possible that this behavior stems from the natural foraging or ground pecking behavior. It has also been noted that a cannibalistic bird will attract more birds in its escape attempts and multiple birds will attack the injured bird. It has been shown that the early experiences of a chick can have an impact on abnormal behaviors in later life. Chicks brooded with a mother have lower incidences of feather pecking and cannibalism than chicks without a mother.

It is believed that the hen guides the chicks to peck at more rewarding items like litter and food. Beak trimming can be used as a method of control but the benefits and disadvantages are the same as mentioned above. Blinders and spectacles have also been used to prevent or restrict cannibalism, but again, these are illegal on welfare grounds in the United Kingdom. Large flock numbers and placing lights in nest boxes can increase the risk of cannibalism. It is believed that the behavior spreads socially in large group numbers. Allowing chicks access to perches by four weeks of age has been associated with reduced cannibalistic risk.

Vent pecking
Vent pecking is when a chicken pecks the vent area of another bird. It causes damage to the cloaca, the skin surrounding it and the tissue underneath. It happens most often after an egg has been laid as the cloaca is partially exposed. It may also be red and bleeding if the egg was over-sized. It is painful and distressing for the attacked bird. It can become cannibalistic and can lead to

disembowelment and death. There are many risk factors in vent pecking. Dim lighting in nest boxes, frequent diet changes during egg laying, stress, bell drinkers, early laying, and disease or immune deficiencies have been attributed as risk factors of vent pecking. It has been suggested that social learning is also a factor. This means that the chickens may learn this behavior from others in the group. It is thought that giving adequate access to perches can reduce incidences of vent pecking. The perches should give each bird enough space, be of adequate height and be facing the feeding area.

Toe pecking
Toe pecking is not as common as other abnormal behaviors but it does occur. This is when one chicken pecks at the toes of another chicken. It can become a cannibalistic behavior and one report has noted fatal incidences. Studies have shown that chickens who exhibit this behavior have enlarged adrenal glands which indicates physiological stress and they also show an increased fear of raised areas.

Feather plucking
Feather plucking differs from feather pecking in that the chicken plucks its own feathers and not those of another chicken. It is also called feather picking, feather damaging behavior and pterotillomania. The bird plucks, chews or bites its own feathers causing damage to the feather and sometimes the skin. It is quite common in parrots but it has been seen in poultry.

The most affected areas are the easily accessible areas such as the wing, flank, chest and neck. It shares some characteristics with trichotillomania which is seen in humans, dogs, cats, mice, guinea pigs, rabbits and sheep. It is caused by inadequate housing and social needs. Stress has also been linked to feather plucking. There may also be neurological or physiological reasons for feather plucking. Improving the environment and social opportunities of the birds can reduce or alleviate feather plucking.

Chapter 11: Behavior

Stereotypies
A stereotypy is a repeated or ritualistic motion or posture. Stereotypies have been linked to inadequate mental stimulation. There are a number of behaviors which are classified as stereotypic behavior including excessive grooming, pacing, rocking, head shaking, self mutilation and excessive sleeping. These behaviors come from artificial environments which deny natural behaviors. These behaviors can be reduced by environmental enrichment and, when possible, allowing the bird or animal to meet its natural behavior needs.

Polydipsia
Polydipsia is excessive water intake. It is not a common abnormal behavior but incidences have been recorded. In some cases, it is the result of the ingestion of toxins. Some foods such as chips, fast food, tinned vegetables, snack foods and crackers, when eaten in abundance can cause salt toxicity which in turn can cause polydipsia. Zinc poisoning has also been known to cause polydipsia. It can also be a symptom of a disease such as diabetes, liver disease, and brain lesions. It can be caused by stress and frustration when the bird is inadequately housed or cared for. Birds who have been subjected to a chronic food restriction have been known to display polydipsia.

Sham dust bathing
Sham dust bathing is when a chicken dust bathes when there is nothing to dust bathe in. Sham dust bathing is exactly like normal dust bathing in that the bird will do exactly what it would in a dust bathing substrate and follow the same patterns. The bird will scratch and peck the ground, fluff the feathers and squat. Then she will lie down and shake the wings, shake her head, rub the beak and scratch with one leg. It is also known as vacuum dust bathing. Konrad Lorenz, a psychologist, performed various experiments on birds and in his theory found that activities like sham dust bathing happened when the need to perform a certain normal behavior - dust bathing - became so great that the bird did it anyway without any of the regular stimuli. It has been noted that birds who dust bathe on wire floors do so near the food. They

appear to treat the food as an appropriate dust bathing substrate. Chickens normal dust bathe every other day. The average dust bath lasts around 27 minutes and generally occurs in the middle of the day. Sham dust bathing follows the same pattern. Chickens who have exhibited sham dust bathing and are then given access to an appropriate substrate, continue to sham dust bathe rather than use the substrate. It has been indicated that stress and frustration in the lack of access to dust bathing results in sham dust bathing as a release. There is also an argument that it is a socially learned behavior, and that chickens learn the behavior from others.

Chronic egg laying
Chronic egg laying can be caused by a variety of factors including environmental and hormonal factors. It can cause egg binding, osteoporosis, hypocalcaemia, feather loss, skin irritation around the cloaca and weight loss. There are several ways of reducing egg laying. Some chicken owners will ask their vet to administer a hormonal injection which will stop egg production. Some chicken owners will leave eggs for the bird to gather a clutch and start nesting. There are fake eggs available which will make the hen believe she has a clutch and start nesting. Some chicken keepers use light manipulation to mimic shorter days. Limiting the access to food can also help slow down or stop egg production but the diet does still need to be completely balanced for a laying hen, as egg production uses a lot of energy.

3) Mating Behavior

Roosters do not have massive changes in plumage when it comes to mating. However, healthy and sexually active males can have firmer combs and wattles which may become darker and more glossy. The feathers may develop more of a sheen or lustre. The rooster does do a courtship 'dance'. He will strut in circles around the hen. It may appear like walking on his tip toes. He may occasionally drag a wing on the ground as he circles. He may present her with food. The hen will crouch down and move her tail feathers to the side to show that she is ready for mating. The roost will mount her back using his beak to hold onto the feathers on her neck and pump his cloaca against hers. Once the mating is complete he will fluff his feathers and walk away. The hen will also fluff her feathers. On occasion, a hen may refuse the rooster. He may accept this and move on or he may forcibly mate with her. This will depend on how many hens are available, his mood and his general personality. Some roosters are very gentle with the hens and will give them food, lead them to nest sites and be gentle during the mating. Other roosters can be rough and only look after themselves. Some roosters will have favorite hens and will mate with them more often than others. Some hens may seduce the rooster and crouch in front of him.

4) Broodiness

All breeds of hen have a surge of hormones about an hour before the laying of an egg. This is when they will look for or build a nest. They will arrange the nest to their liking. They will make crooning sounds and may sit on the nest for a few minutes after the egg has been laid. When the hen becomes broody, the surge of hormones doesn't reduce much after the egg is laid. For the first five days, the hen will stay close to the nest but not actually nest. She will feel protective of the eggs there and will defend them from anything she perceives as a threat. After she has laid five to ten eggs, she will sit on the nest and incubate the eggs. She will only eat and drink when she feels safe and feels that her nest is safe.

Chapter 12: Eggs

1) Collecting the Eggs

The eggs will need to be collected often. It is a good idea to collect them 2 to 3 times per day. Doing this helps prevent against breakages. When collecting eggs it is best to put them in a basket or buckets which has bedding or some other soft material which will prevent the eggs from smashing into each other and the sides. If the birds are free range, they may try to hide the eggs. Dirty eggs can be cleaned. You can use a cloth to brush off the dirt. However, if the egg is very dirty, then some chicken owners advise against using them if they have been laid in areas which are extremely dirty. While it is fine to clean off some eggs, it is important not to routinely wash your eggs. Doing this can remove some of the natural protection of the shell that helps protect the freshness. Eggs should be storage in enclosed clean boxes as enclosed boxes keep them fresh for longer than open boxes. The eggs should be put with pointed end downwards into the box. After they have been boxed they should be refrigerated.

2) Quality of Eggs

The eggs which are sold in stores are produced on a large commercial scale and are graded according to the exterior and interior quality of the egg. Shells must be unbroken for all the grades. The grading system determines where the eggs will end up. The lower grade eggs are most often used for egg products such as dried egg whites. Eggs which do not fit one of the grading categories are not suitable for human consumption. Although it is unnecessary to grade eggs laid at home, there are guidelines to help assess the quality of backyard eggs.

Chapter 12: Eggs

Firstly the exterior is assessed in terms of its cleanliness and its strength. This is because the appearance of the eggs is the first thing anybody sees. The cleanliness of the shell is important to protect against bacterial contamination. If the shell is clean, the more it can protect against bacteria. The strength of the shell determines the ability of the egg to stay intact. The shell is about 12% of the weight of the egg. It is made of three layers. The inner layer covers the inner and outer membranes.

The next layer in the egg is a spongy layer which is made of about 94% calcium carbonate.This layer forms pores which connects the surface of the inner and outer shell and allows carbon dioxide to leave the egg. The third layer is known as the bloom or the cuticle. This is a coating which seals the pores and helps preserve the freshness. It does this by preventing bacteria from entering through the shell. Washing the eggs can remove the bloom. Commercial egg farms will spray the eggs with a film of oil which can make the eggs appear shiny. If it is necessary to wash home laid eggs, then rubbing the dried egg with clean vegetable oil can replace the bloom which was removed by washing. It is the shape of the egg as well as the composition that gives the strength.

In terms of composition it is influenced directly from the diet and the age of the hen. This means that the eggs of an older hen have weaker and thinner shells. The shape of the egg means that the two (ends??) are strong but the middle is weak enough to allow a chick to hatch. The shell of an egg has no value for human consumption. However shells can be given as a calcium supplement to chickens, added to compost, added to soil for tomatoes or used for arts and crafts.

The quality of the interior of the egg is assessed by the appearance and consistency. There is more than one type of egg white. One of them is the firm white around the yolk and another is a thinner white closer to the shell. There is an inner thin-layer between the yolk and the whites.

3) Freshness

Sometimes it can be difficult to be sure how long ago an egg was laid. There are a few methods of estimating the freshness of an egg. The first is a process known as candling. This means that the egg is viewed in front of a strong light. Originally this was done in front of a candle which is where the name comes from. Lights which have been designed especially for this are available to buy but a small flashlight with a strong bulb works just as well. Beginners to candling should practice with white eggs before colored eggs because the darker color is much more difficult to see through. In a dark room hold the egg between two fingers and at a slant with the larger end tilted towards the light. Turn your wrist towards the contents of the egg. The white of a fresh egg is dense, the yolk should look vague and fuzzy. The white grows thinner as the egg ages. A thinner white does not anchor the yolk which means that it can move closer to the shell. The size of the air cell increases with age. The cell of a fresh egg is no bigger than 3 mm or about an eighth of an inch. If the cell is bigger than that then the egg is not fresh. It is possible to estimate the freshness of an egg based on the size of the cell.

Another method is to float the egg in water. A fresh egg will lie on the bottom of the container horizontally. A week old egg will rise up slightly at the larger end. If the egg is 2 to 3 weeks old then it will stand vertically with the big end upwards. If the egg can float this means that the cell has grown big enough to make the egg buoyant. This does not necessarily mean that the egg is unfit for human consumption.

The quickest method of determining whether or not an egg can be eaten is by the smell. A rotten egg gives off a foul smelling gas called hydrogen sulfide. This is also known as rotten egg gas. If an egg smells bad, whether it is raw or cooked, it should be immediately disposed of.

Visually examining the contents of a broken egg is another method. The white of a fresh egg should look cloudy. The whites can

Chapter 12: Eggs

become clear and transparent because, as the egg ages, the gas escapes. The white of an older egg can be watery and does not support the yolk very well. The yolk of an older egg may have a weakened membrane which can cause the yolk to break.

4) *Abnormalities in Eggs*

Abnormalities in eggs can be random, hereditary, or due to other management and/or environmental factors. Abnormalities can be detected by visible examination and by candling.

Wind eggs
Egg without the yolk are known as dwarf or wind eggs. These can be quite common in the first lay of a pullet. This is because the internal system for egg laying is not fully prepared. It is possible for wind eggs to appear in mature birds but this is rare. The cause of wind eggs in a mature hen is usually tissue which has broken away and has been treated like a yolk. These eggs were sometimes known as cock eggs because people believed that they were laid by roosters.

Double yolks
Eggs with two yolks can appear if the bird of ovulates too quickly or if a yolk moves too slowly and a second yolk catches up with it. Sometimes these eggs can be laid by pullets because the production cycle may not be completely synchronized. Some breeds lay these eggs as a hereditary trait. Very occasionally there may be more than two yolks in the egg.

Double shell
Another abnormality in eggs is a double shell. This is also known as an egg within an egg. This happens when an egg that is almost ready to be laid reverses and gets re-covered in shell. There is no definitive explanation as to why this abnormality happens.

Blood spots
Blood spots are blood which has been released with the yolk. This happens from a small ruptured blood vessel. This abnormality has

no effect on the suitability of the egg for human consumption. The developing yolk is stored inside a sac where blood vessels supply the necessary substances for maturation. The yolk is then most often released from a section of the sac which has no blood vessels. This is called the stigma of suture line. Sometimes the sac can rupture which causes vessels to break and blood to appear in the egg. As the egg ages the blood spots become paler. This abnormality is more common in older birds. There are two possible explanations for blood spots. They might be caused by a deficiency of vitamin A or they might be hereditary.

Meat spots
Meat spots are not as common as blood spots. They have no effect on human consumption but can look off putting. It is possible that they started as a blood spot which changed color due to chemical reactions or they may have been a tissue particle. It is believed they are hereditary. They can be white, gray, tan, brown, or red brown. This 'explanation' doesn't really say much – where do they occur?

Wormy eggs
If the birds have high parasite burdens it is possible for worms to be in the egg. This is extremely rare and highly off putting. It is a clear indication that the birds need to be wormed.
Eggs with a strange flavor can be a result of the diet. Onions, garlic, fruit peel, fish meal, excessive flax seeds and, or, fish oil can make the flavor of the egg unpleasant. Unpleasant taste can also come from odors. If the eggs are stored near kerosene, carbolic acid, molds, mustiness, fruit and vegetables then they may absorb the odor, which can affect the taste.

Developing embryo
If the egg has been partially incubated, there may be a developing embryo inside. This can happen when the birds hide the nests. It may be the result of the egg being incubated each time the hen lays a new egg or it may indicate that the bird started to sit on the eggs but abandoned the incubation attempt.

Chapter 12: Eggs

5) *Egg Safety*

Eggs can attract bacteria and mold because a fresh laid egg is warm and moist. To help prevent bacteria from entering the egg through the pores, it is important to make sure that the nest boxes are clean and have fresh litter. It is unlikely for eggs from a clean environment, which are refrigerated quickly and collected twice daily, to cause illness to humans after consumption. If the egg is cracked but the membrane is intact and the egg is used immediately, it is safe to eat. This is known as a check egg. If there is leakage from a cracked egg then the membrane has broken and the egg should be disposed of.

It is possible to clean dirty eggs but any seriously dirty eggs should be disposed of. If the egg is slightly dirty it can be washed. Washing can remove the bloom so a washed egg can be sanitized by dipping in a solution of 1 teaspoon of chlorine bleach mixed in 1 quarts (2 pints) of warm water. The egg should be dipped for a maximum of 30 seconds. The egg must be then dried. Rubbing the egg with clean vegetable oil can act as a replacement bloom. It should then be put in an egg box and refrigerated. Eggs can keep in a household fridge for about five weeks.

There are some bacteria which are able to survive on the shell. They may die during storage but can be replaced by other strains of bacteria. Some of these bacteria can cause eggs to rot. There are also molds which can survive on eggshell. These molds can penetrate the egg and cause rot.

Salmonella can be on the interior or exterior of an egg. Bacteria can cause serious illness when consumed. The bacteria can multiply if the egg is stored at an incorrect temperature. Thoroughly cooking eggs destroys any risk of salmonella poisoning. Eggs should be cooked slowly so as to ensure that they are heated all the way through. Any hot foods with eggs as an ingredient should be kept at 140°F (60°C) or warmer. Any cold foods with egg ingredients should be stored at 40°F (4°C) or colder.

Chapter 12: Eggs

Here are some tips to help avoid food poisoning:
The eggs should be collected often.
The eggs should be refrigerated as soon as possible.
After handling raw eggs hands and utensils should be thoroughly washed.
Any foods which have been made with raw or under cooked eggs need to be refrigerated immediately.
Eggs and egg-based foods should be cooked to 160°F (71°C) and served immediately. They can also be quickly cooled and refrigerated.
Leftovers should be refrigerated as soon as possible and used within four days.

6) Nutritional Value of Eggs

A large egg is approximately 31% yolk, 58% white and 11% shell. It contains about 12% protein and 12% fat. The yolk itself contains proteins, fat, pigments and other minor nutrients and vitamins. Most of the egg's cholesterol and calorie values are also in the yolk. The yolk contains lecithin which acts as an emulsion when making mayonnaise and hollandaise sauce. There has been some evidence which suggests that the same substance may improve memory.
The egg white is made up of water and several different types of protein. Egg protein is considered to be complete as it contains all essential amino acids. A large egg contains approximately 6.25 g of protein which is about the equivalent of one ounce or 28 g of lean meat fish legumes or poultry. It also contains a protein called avidin. Some people (?? "including pregnant women and the elderly") can be sensitive to this protein and therefore should not be routinely fed raw eggs. However a person would have to eat 24 eggs per day to be affected. Cooking the egg deactivates?? this protein.

Some people believe that fertilized eggs have more nutritional value than unfertilized eggs. However the sperm which fertilizes an egg contributes an insignificant amount of nutrition. There is also a belief that the color of the shell changes the nutritional value. It is believed that colored eggs are more nutritious than white eggs.

Chapter 12: Eggs

However, it is not the color that affects nutritional value, but rather how the egg is produced. Free range eggs contain more nutrition than caged eggs. If the birds have access to pasture or green feed then the egg will contain less cholesterol and saturated fat and (?? more)vitamin A, D and E, beta-carotene, folic acid and omega-3 polyunsaturated fatty acid. Feeding flax seed to the birds can also increase the amount of omega-3 in the egg.

7) Problems in Egg Laying

On occasion some birds may produce less eggs than expected or may not produce eggs. There are several problems which can affect the production of eggs. Some hens also develop a liking to eggs and prefer to eat them themselves than have the chicken owner collect them. If you're having problems with the egg production, you need to find out which birds are not laying and why they are not.

Common reasons for problems in egg laying
While a bird who is not laying may be suffering from a physical injury or a genetic problem, it is much more likely that problems in the laying are a result of incorrect management.
One of the most common reasons is that all the birds are actually roosters. This can happen if you purchase a blind run of chicks. This means that the chicks have not been sexed and is a generally cheaper option when purchasing your birds. However, it can be common for chicken owners to end up with an abundance of roosters.

Another common reason is that the bird is simply too young to begin egg laying. The different breeds have different rates of maturation and while many of the egg laying breeds can begin laying at 18 weeks old, some breeds do take longer to mature and begin egg production. It is important to give your birds time to start their egg producing lives.

It is also possible that the bird is too old. After about three years of age, many birds either stop laying completely or lay only a few

Chapter 12: Eggs

eggs. This can be a risk when purchasing adult birds but chickens do not show any obvious signs of aging, which makes it quite difficult to age the birds accurately.

If the birds are not getting the correct nutrition from their food then they probably won't lay. The hormones which control the laying cycle and egg production will not function properly without the proper balance of vitamins and minerals. Chickens will only eat what they need to meet their energy requirements and if the food is of poor quality or not nutritionally correct, then it may affect egg production.
Birds suffering from illness can stop laying completely. It can be difficult to detect illness in chickens as they will try to hide the symptoms until the illness is severe.

It is also possible that stress is keeping the birds from egg laying. On occasion the birds will be able to adjust to whatever is causing stress and begin laying or the caretaker can remove the source of stress and the birds will begin egg laying.
If you are sure that the cessation of egg production is not because of any of the above reasons, then it could be a good idea to have an experienced chicken owner or a vet check the birds.

Finding out which bird has the problem
When you look at a hen who is laying next to a hen who is not laying there are differences. The comb, earlobes and wattles of laying birds are bright, shiny and plump whereas in non-laying birds they are small, pale, dry and not as fleshy. Also the vent of a laying bird is large and moist but it is small and dry in a bird who is not laying. The pelvic bones of a laying hen are spaced further apart than a non-laying hen. If a bird who is not laying is healthy, she can look a little more sleek and plump because there is no energy spent on making eggs. If the bird is an older bird or if it is sick it can look fluffed up, inactive and drowsy. The behavior of the birds can also indicate which of them are laying and which of them are not. Generally hens who are not laying and are not broody, do not spend a lot of time around the nest boxes. Broody hens will spend all their time on a nest. Hens can make a lot of noise when

Chapter 12: Eggs

they lay so if there is a hen near a nest box who is making a lot of noise in the morning, it is probable that it is laying.

Another way of determining which of the birds is not laying is to pen them singly with the nest box until midday. This will need to be done for several days before any conclusions can be reached. It is also possible that the birds are not laying in the nest box. Free range birds may choose to lay in other places so if the birds are free range, it is important to make sure all areas are searched before concluding that there is a problem.

Free range layers and problem layers
Free range birds can and will lay wherever they choose. This means that the caretaker may have to search for the eggs. But there are other birds who, regardless of the availability of nests, lay eggs wherever they happen to be at the time. If the nest boxes are comfortable and clean but the birds are laying eggs from the perch or on the floor, then it can be a result of a hormone deficiency. It may also be partially due to habit. Keeping the birds penned until around midday with plenty of available nest boxes will usually be helpful with this problem.

About an hour before the egg is laid, the bird will have a raise in hormone levels which should make her want to seek a nest to lay the egg in. After the egg has been laid, the hormone levels drop and the nest no longer holds any interest for the bird. If all nest boxes are in use or if the bird has a particular box that she prefers, she can delay laying but after a certain amount of time the hormone levels will drop regardless and the bird will no longer care to look for a nest box and will lay the eggs wherever she happens to be.

However when there are plenty of nest boxes and a bird is laying all over the place, it can be related to a hormone deficiency. This tends to be a bigger problem with high production egg laying breeds in comparison to other breeds. Some chicken owners prefer to keep the birds penned until laying is completed. Access to a fenced outdoor run can be allowed but if they start laying outside often, the best idea is to keep them inside and ensure that there is no

Chapter 12: Eggs

problem with the nest boxes. It is also a good idea to keep young birds in a fenced area until they had established a routine for egg laying and good habits. Birds who are new to the flock should also be kept inside until they are used to their new surroundings.

Free range birds will find their own place outside for laying. Despite laying outside, the birds will probably return to the coop at night. The nests of free range chickens can be particularly hard to find and the rooster may actually help the hens to find safe, secure and secluded areas to nest.

Broody birds and laying
When a hen has a clutch of eggs she will stop laying and begin to incubate the eggs. She will begin laying when the chicks are raised or if the eggs haven't hatched. There are several old wives' tale methods of stopping a hen from going broody. However, these methods do not work and are cruel. Broodiness is hormonal and doing things like throwing cold water on a bird, making the lights brighter, scaring her off the nest or putting her under a basket have no effect on the hormones. It is the hormone levels which will determine when a bird stops attempting to incubate eggs.

If a bird is trying to incubate eggs, most chicken owners just continue to collect them. The eggs cannot be left with the hen for more than a few hours. She will continue to lay to attempt to replace the missing ones. After this she may abandon the nest, stop laying eggs for a short while and then returning to her normal rate of a production. Or alternatively, she may try to incubate an empty nest. Most owners believe it is best to leave her be, and in about three weeks she'll give up. Occasionally some birds will begin to go broody almost immediately. There are three options in this event. The first is to remove her from the flock and replace her with a new bird. The second is to allow her to incubate fertilized eggs and raise the chicks. The third is to let her incubate an empty nest until she gives up.

Breaking and eating eggs
This problem is the least frequent of common causes of a decline in

Chapter 12: Eggs

egg production. However, it can spread quickly through the flock because birds will copy rewarding behavior. Before determining that it is the chickens who are breaking and eating the eggs, it is important to rule out other animals. The animals who do this are usually nocturnal so all eggs should be collected before nightfall. Any eggs that have been smashed need to be cleaned up immediately. Never feed raw eggs to the birds, but they can be fed if cooked and mashed beforehand. If feeding eggshell to the birds, it needs to be crushed and ground into very small pieces so as to look nothing like eggs.

It is unlikely for this problem to occur in a free range flock. Free range birds are much less likely to stay near the nest boxes and eat the eggs. Confined birds do not have the same space and can be bored which can result in egg eating. It is generally thought that feeding a good quality balanced feed and supplementing with crushed oyster shell provides the birds with proteins and minerals which can make eating eggs unnecessary. Other chicken owners put plastic or ceramic eggs in the nest. This can make the hens give up the habit of egg eating as they cannot break the fake eggs. However, this does not work in all cases.

Chapter 13: Gardening With Chickens

Chickens can be both a help and a hindrance in the garden. The foraging behavior can damage the roots of the plants. There are a few ways to chicken proof the garden. Some chicken owners believe that as long as there is an abundance of space for the birds then they will be less likely to destroy plants. However, vegetable plots and flower beds can be fenced off to prevent the chickens from getting access. Large stones around the base of a plant can discourage scratching. A mesh covering can be used to protect young plants. Some chicken owners recommend planting a garden especially for the chickens with low bushes and berries for them to peck at.

1) Chickens and Pests

Chickens can be very enthusiastic pest controllers. They will eat grasshoppers, slugs, snails and various beetles. They will eat the adult insect and will scratch the ground to find the larvae. Some chicken owners recommend fencing the vegetable area off but allowing the chickens in, as long as young plantings are protected, for around an hour per day. before sun set. The time limit means that the chickens don't have time to do serious damage to the plants. Other chicken owners recommend keeping them out of the garden from spring until fall, only allowing access in winter. Chicken will also scratch through a compost heap and control the pests there as well. Their manure can be beneficial to some plants and can increase the nutrients of home made compost. This will depend on your location as some areas prohibit using chicken manure, as it can pollute water sources. If your chickens will have garden access then it is important to use a pesticide which is non-toxic and safe for the chickens

Chapter 13: Gardening With Chickens

2) Dangerous Plants

Some plants can be toxic to animals and birds. These include daffodils, morning glory, common St. John's Wort, laburnum seeds, castor bean, mountain laurel, corn cockle, black nightshade, hen bane, yew, most irises, rhododendron, oleander, yew, castor bean, clematis, rapeseed, sweet pea, meadow buttercup, foxglove, vetch, ragwort and some fungi, jimsonweed weed, tulips, azaleas, rhododendron, monkshood, amaryllis, lily of the valley, potato sprouts, trumpet vine, nightshade, nicotiana, privet, rhubarb leaves and tansy. There may be other plants found in your area which are not listed here. It is a good idea to limit the access your birds have to any plant which could harm them.

3) Vermin

Chickens will attract rats. The rats will enjoy the chicken feed and will eat as much of it as they can. The gestation period of a rat is about three weeks and litter sizes are around ten babies. A female can have around five litters a year and females are ready to reproduce at four months old. Rats can multiply quickly and become a problem. Correct food storage can help keep the chicken food safe. Cats can control rat population. However, cats will also need to be fed and looked after. Some people believe that female cats are better at hunting than males. Depending on the gun laws in your area, shooting the rats is also an option. However, rats can move quickly and the shooter may miss them. Rat poison is available to buy. Care must be taken to ensure that it is not accessible by pets and children. There are also rat traps available or a professional pest control service can come and do the pest control for you. Dead rats should be disposed of immediately.

Websites and Resources

Please note that I have not bought any chickens from these websites mentioned in the book. Make sure that you investigate breeders very well before you buy any chickens from them. There are a lot of scammers on the web simply trading to make money and they do not care at all about the chicken's health and safety.

UNITED STATES

Murray McMurray Hatchery Iowa
www.mcmurrayhatchery.com

Cackle Hatchery , Lebanon
www.cacklehatchery.com

Meyer Hatchery, Polk
www.meyerhatchery.com

American Poultry Association
www.amerpoultryassn.com/

CANADA

Berg's Hatchery Box 5
www.bergshatchery.com
www.rochesterhatchery.com

Poultry Industry Council
www.poultryindustrycouncil.ca

UNITED KINGDOM

Horton Hatchery
Leighton Buzzard
www.hortonhatchery.co.uk

Websites and Resources

Farmgate Hatchery
www.farmgatehatcheries.com

The Poultry Farm,
Preston,
www.tombarron.co.uk

Poultry Club
www.poultryclub.org

The British Poultry Council
www.britishpoultry.org.uk

AUSTRALIA

Barter and Sons Hatchery, Luddenham

Wagner's Poultry, Coldstream
www.wagnerspoultry.com.au

Altona Hatchery, Forrestfield
www.altona.net.au

South Australian Poultry Association
www.sapoultryassoc.org.au

Rare Poultry Breeders Association
www.rarepoultrybreedersassociation.com

NEW ZEALAND

Heslips Hatchery, South Canterbury
www.heslipshatcheries.co.nz

New Zealand Poultry Association
www.nzpoultryassociationsinc.co.nz

Published by IMB Publishing 2014

Copyright and Trademarks. This publication is Copyright 2014 by IMB Publishing. All products, publications, software and services mentioned and recommended in this publication are protected by trademarks. In such instance, all trademarks & copyright belong to the respective owners. All rights reserved. No part of this book may be reproduced or transferred in any form or by any means, graphic, electronic, or mechanical, including photocopying, recording, taping, or by any information storage retrieval system, without the written permission of the author. Pictures used in this book are either royalty free pictures bought from stock-photo websites or have the source mentioned underneath the picture.

Disclaimer and Legal Notice.   This product is not legal or medical advice and should not be interpreted in that manner. You need to do your own due-diligence to determine if the content of this product is right for you. The author and the affiliates of this product are not liable for any damages or losses associated with the content in this product. While every attempt has been made to verify the information shared in this publication, neither the author nor the affiliates assume any responsibility for errors, omissions or contrary interpretation of the subject matter herein.   Any perceived slights to any specific person(s) or organization(s) are purely unintentional. We have no control over the nature, content and availability of the web sites listed in this book. The inclusion of any web site links does not necessarily imply a recommendation or endorse the views expressed within them. IMB Publishing takes no responsibility for, and will not be liable for, the websites being temporarily unavailable or being removed from the Internet. The accuracy and completeness of information provided herein and opinions stated herein are not guaranteed or warranted to produce any particular results, and the advice and strategies, contained herein may not be suitable for every individual. The author shall not be liable for any loss incurred as a consequence of the use and application, directly or indirectly, of any information presented in this work. This publication is designed to provide information in regard to the subject matter covered. The information included in this book has been compiled to give an overview of the subjects and detail some of the symptoms, treatments etc. that are available to canines with these conditions. It is not intended to give medical advice. For a firm diagnosis of your dog's condition, and for a treatment plan suitable for you, you should consult your veterinarian or consultant. The writer of this book and the publisher are not responsible for any damages or negative consequences following any of the treatments or methods highlighted in this book. Website links are for informational purposes only and should not be seen as a personal endorsement; the same applies to the products detailed in this book. The reader should also be aware that although the web links included were correct at the time of writing, they may become out of date in the future.

www.ingramcontent.com/pod-product-compliance
Lightning Source LLC
Chambersburg PA
CBHW060836050426
42453CB00008B/714